The Art of

Being YOU

I0531771

An Enneagram Journey to Discovering
Personality Type, Self-Awareness, and
Personal Growth

Richard Banks

Why You Should Read This Book

We are all searching for resolutions to the challenges we face. Even if we don't always communicate it directly, we all want to help ourselves and others and enjoy fuller, more satisfying lives. The Enneagram may not be able to solve every problem. Still, it can shine a light on why and how so many individuals inflict misery upon themselves and, by extension, others around them. The Enneagram personality types reveal the most prominent aspects of our inner geography, including the locations of our soul's perilous cliffs, deserts, and deadly quicksand, as well as its nourishing oases, tranquil forests, and revitalizing springs. We may choose whether or not to explore such depths, risk the pitfalls of emotional quicksand, or travel into uncharted territories. When the Enneagram is correctly understood and used, it becomes a map that shows us where we are in terms of our personalities and where we may go after we've gotten over ourselves.

Humans are incredibly complex, wonderful,

infuriating, adaptable, and puzzling. It's as true about yourself as it is about the dozens of people you bump into daily. Every time you interact with others, you must operate on the often very limited knowledge you have about them.

And so much of it comes back to two fundamental problems:

We don't truly understand others.
We don't even truly understand ourselves.

This is why understanding personality can be so incredibly helpful. Personality typology is one of the personal and social constructs we've discovered to significantly influence our lives. No theory or framework can adequately describe or wholly account for who you are.

There are reasons why people behave the way they do. Having a method to put those reasons into a more transparent system will allow you to grow your empathy and compassion for others. But much more importantly, understanding your reasons for doing what you do will grow compassion for yourself! And not just that, it will also give you the chance to do something about it.

Because you cannot change what you're not aware of.

This has made the Enneagram such a helpful tool for self-transformation for millions of people. The Enneagram is a personality typing system comprising nine unique personality types. It can be a valuable and profound tool for personal growth that helps build empathy and understanding for ourselves and others. The Enneagram invites us to look deeply into the mystery of our true identity. It is meant to initiate a process of inquiry that can lead us to a more profound truth about ourselves and our place in the world.

The Enneagram is best used as a guide to self-observation and self-inquiry. The Enneagram allows you to see some of the most difficult parts of yourself that you can't see without intentional reflection. It gives you a blueprint for understanding why you act the way you do. And if you can do the hard work and look at those blueprints, you will finally have what you need to begin growing in a long-lasting, transformative way.

This book will teach you:

- How to "observe and let go" of troublesome habits and reactions
- How to work with the motivations of each type
- Unconscious childhood messages
- Therapeutic strategies for each type
- How to cultivate awareness in your daily life
- How to use the system for continuing spiritual growth

This book will help you understand how you react to other people and experiences in your life and what those reactions tell you about your stress level and overall emotional health. When you understand yourself better, you can stop being controlled by fear and start living the life you desire.

It is time for us all to stop living in the past and realize our full potential. If you want to live an authentic life full of meaning and fulfillment, this book is for you! It will help you understand how your reactions to different situations can tell you about your overall emotional health and challenges. Utilize the information in this book to become the most improved version of yourself you can be. The world is counting on each of us to show up, to be less preoccupied with our egos, and to infect the social ecosystem with the most brilliant ideas we can muster.

Thank You!

Thank you for your purchase.

I am dedicated to making the most enriching and informational content. I hope it meets your expectations and you gain a lot from it.

Your comments and feedback are important to me because they help me to provide the best material possible. So, if you have any questions or concerns, please email me at richardbanks.books@gmail.com.

Again, thank you for your purchase.

INTRODUCTION

I would like to ask a question—how would you characterize yourself? Who are you?

Since the beginning of human history, people have been hard at work developing personal and social constructs to define our personalities. These constructs consist of our many faiths, beliefs, meditative practices, and political structures. As a result, we arrange ourselves and our knowledge into what Timothy Leary would term "reality tunnels." These tunnels are our preferred ways of seeing the world, and we attempt to remain in harmony with these tunnels as much as possible.

We are all driven by a profound inner yearning. We may feel this yearning as a sense that something is missing in us, although it is usually difficult to define exactly what it is. We all have different ideas about what we think we need or want—a better relationship, a better job, a better body, a better home, and so on. We believe that if we get that perfect relationship or job or new "toy," the yearning will go away, and we will feel satisfied and complete. But experience teaches us that the new car makes us feel better for only a short time. The new relationship may be amazing, but it never quite fulfills us as we thought it would. So what are we really looking for? If we reflect for a moment, we may realize that what our hearts yearn for is to know who we are and why we are here. But little in our culture encourages us to hunt for answers to these essential questions. We've been brought up to believe that our exterior conditions will have the most impact on how happy we are. Sooner or later, however, we realize that superficial pleasures, while valuable in themselves, cannot address the deep restlessness of our soul. So, where can we look for answers?

Most personal development books on the market today focus primarily on the type of individuals we aspire to be. They recognize the vital importance of empathy, leadership, communication, and creativity. But as important and attractive as these (and other) qualities are, we find it extremely difficult to maintain them or to put them into practice in our daily lives. Our hearts yearn to soar, yet we almost always come crashing down painfully on the rocks of fear, self-defeating habits, and misinformation.

An effective approach to personal development must consider the fact that there are different kinds of people—different personality types. Personality typology is one of the personal and social constructs we've discovered to significantly influence our lives. No theory or framework can adequately describe or wholly account for who you are—the human species is too complicated to fit into one single framework, as there are so many things to be considered.

Learning about one facet of your personality doesn't magically reduce you to being only that aspect of yourself, any more than standing on a map would magically move you to a certain area. However, personality typology has proven to be one of the most valuable guides we've encountered in our search for self. Your personality might not be a direct indication of who you are, but it can serve as a map or guide to help you figure that out. And it is my conviction that our personalities may serve not only as a map to help us discover who we already are, but also as a manual to assist us in developing into the people we want to be.

No matter how well you're doing in life, the truth is that every person begins life affected in some way by the people around us and our experiences. And each one of us, consciously or unconsciously, covered over or clouded our true self, that fragrant essence of who we really are, devoid of all the clutter we picked up along the way.

This book will help you understand how you react to other people and experiences in your life and what those reactions tell you about your stress level and overall emotional health. When you understand yourself better, you can stop being controlled by fear and start living the life you desire.

Let's be honest—we're all a little lost sometimes. We go through life thinking that if we just had more money, more friends, or more time, everything would be okay. But the truth is that money, friends, and time are not what we need most. What we really need is to understand ourselves better.

Have you ever wondered why you sometimes feel stuck in the same patterns, repeating the same mistakes over and over? Or why sometimes you feel like you're constantly struggling to keep up with everyone else?

It's because we've been indoctrinated with false beliefs about ourselves and our reality.

No matter where we come from, our false beliefs about ourselves and our reality greatly limit our growth and evolution. We become empowered by embracing our fears, uncovering false beliefs, and seeing others like us who have broken these patterns. We spend so much time trying to determine our personality type and how it affects us. We ask ourselves if we're extroverted or introverted, or if we're a thinker or a feeler. We ask ourselves where we fall on the spectrum of introversion/extroversion and whether we're more of a judger or a perceiver.

Because when you get down to it, all these labels— introvert/extrovert, thinker/feeler, judger/perceiver— are just constructs that we as humans have made up over time to try to understand ourselves and each other better. And while they might seem like helpful tools for understanding yourself, they can also blind you from seeing your full potential as a human being.

Coaching all over the world has taught me that we are all indoctrinated with false pretenses that do not serve us. We must break the old patterns and awaken to our true potential.

We are not our beliefs! When we believe this, we limit ourselves and others from experiencing the fullness of life. Our beliefs blind and limit us, holding us to a limited perspective. Our thoughts hold us back from experiencing life without limitations, without fear of judgment or failure, and without the need for approval. Our past and future thoughts keep us from enjoying the present moment.

We have the clarity to see through these false pretenses and what others are trying to teach us and mirror for us. We can step outside of this limited perspective with an awareness that allows us to grow into our fullest potential as human beings.

What if there were a system that could enable us to have more insight into ourselves and others? What if this system could show us our core psychological issues as well as our strengths and weaknesses? What if this system did not depend on the assertions of experts or gurus, but on our personality patterns and willingness to explore ourselves honestly? What if this system showed us not only our core issues but also pointed out effective ways of dealing with them? Such a system exists, and it is called the Enneagram.

The Enneagram is a clear map of our souls for personal empowerment. It shows us exactly where we've been and where we're going in life—and helps us get there faster and with less struggle than ever before. In other words, it is a personality typology that maps the nine different types of personalities. Each type has its strengths and weaknesses, and each has its unique way of being in the world.

Knowing our type can help us discover how we operate in the world, why we do what we do, and what motivates us. The Enneagram is here to help you better understand yourself and live your best life! It can help us to understand ourselves, our relationships, and the world around us in a new way.

It's also an excellent tool for personal empowerment.

This tool helps us better understand the motives behind our behaviors by identifying nine different personality types. Each type has a unique way of approaching life and interacting with others. It is a tool to discover, understand, and live with our true selves.

It's a modern tool that uses ancient ideas to help you

take charge of your life.

The Enneagram shows us how to be better versions of ourselves by understanding what drives us, what holds us back, and how we can best use our strengths to help us achieve our goals. If you're a little confused right now, don't worry—that's all part of the process! The purpose of determining your Enneagram personality type is not to put yourself in a box but to identify the box you habitually put yourself in and step outside of it with awareness so that you can grow into your fullest potential as a human being.

Here's the gist—even with the most healthy, supportive parents on the planet, you will end up masking, suppressing, denying, or clouding parts of your true self or essence. Then you'll spend the rest of your life feeling like you're missing some important pieces of the puzzle you have become. Thus it becomes your lifelong quest to unveil your essence and become who you were meant to be. The Enneagram is a great road map to the treasures that lie inside you— unexpressed or expressed, conscious or unconscious, underutilized or unclaimed, and ripe with essence.

The veil becomes your personality and consists of what you think and feel and how you act or react to various life situations. The way you process information, as well as the way you characteristically behave, creates an amalgam of personality traits that define who you are. The Enneagram delineates nine core personality types and elucidates each type's primary fixations, motivations, and behavior patterns. Because everyone is born with certain affinities and is greatly affected by their formative years, variations within each type can be wide-ranging. Adult life experiences also affect personality alteration, accounting for swings in one direction or another. The Enneagram identifies nine core personalities based on the primary or predominant way people of each type emotionally experience, look at, and interact with the world around them. The Enneagram differs from other personality typing systems in that it doesn't describe our behaviors. There are stereotypical behaviors that align with each of the nine types, but the Enneagram is about our motivations—the *why* and *how* behind what we do. We all may exhibit the same behaviors, but the motivations behind those behaviors are often very different. Those motivations are what delineate the nine different types.

It's a natural human instinct to want to know more about ourselves. We want to understand who we are, why we are like this, how we got here, and how we can move forward. We strive to know ourselves a little bit more today than we did yesterday. You're not alone, and you no longer have to live with stress, anxiety, and fear. In this book, you'll learn how to understand your reactions to life events so that you can stop being controlled by fear and start living the life of your dreams.

One important idea in our understanding of the Enneagram is the importance of self-awareness and introspection to progress toward personal growth and development. Acquiring in-depth knowledge of ourselves is the first step in altering our behavior and transcending our "false personality." Every spiritual journey begins with an individual's ability to transcend their ego, and the Enneagram reveals this process for each personality type. The Enneagram inspires us to explore ego transcendence and the integration of higher levels of consciousness by revealing the freer, broader dimensions of our own being and reassuring us that they are within our reach.

We are all searching for resolutions to the challenges we face. Even if we don't always communicate it directly, we all want to help ourselves and others and enjoy fuller, more satisfying lives. The Enneagram may not be able to solve every problem. Still, it can shine a light on why and how so many individuals inflict misery upon themselves and, by extension, others around them. The Enneagram personality types reveal the most prominent aspects of our inner geography, including the locations of our soul's perilous cliffs, deserts, and deadly quicksands, as well as its nourishing oases, tranquil forests, and revitalizing springs. We may choose whether or not to explore such depths, risk the pitfalls of emotional quicksand, or travel into uncharted territories. When the Enneagram is correctly understood and used, it becomes a map that shows us where we are in terms of our personalities and where we may go after we've gotten over ourselves.

If you want to live an authentic life full of meaning and

fulfillment, this book is for you! It will help you understand how your reactions to different situations can tell you about your overall emotional health and challenges. Once you have that information, you can learn how to stop being controlled by fear and start living the life you desire.

The Enneagram helps us understand and express our innate individuality. We believe every person has a unique combination of characteristics, and we have created this book to help you find your unique mix. Determining our Enneagram personality type isn't meant to label us but rather to help us see the limitations of our worldview and break free of them so that we may develop to our maximum potential. In *The Art of Being You*, we'll help you discover what makes you YOU—and how to use those strengths to create the life YOU want!

It is time for us all to stop living in the past and realize our full potential. The Enneagram provides a transparent road map to our inner strengths and potential. Utilize the information in this book to become the most improved version of yourself you can be. The world is counting on each of us to show up, to be less preoccupied with our egos, and to infect the social ecosystem with the most brilliant ideas we can muster.

Let's begin!

CHAPTER 1: HOW PERSONALITY IS FORMED

*"All of our experiences fuse into our personality.
Everything that ever happened to us is an
ingredient."* – Anonymous

In normal daily discourse, personality comes up rather often. For example, "You have such a wonderful personality!" Or, you may say something like, "This is my personality—take it or leave it."

You are the product of your environment. Your personality is formed as a complex interplay between inborn traits and characteristics and your life experiences. But you're also born with specific personality attributes that can shape how you respond to your environment and how it responds back. These two factors work together to create a unique individual who stands out from others.

Personality is a complicated thing. People are often born with a dominant personality type and assume it's up to their environment to shape them into something else. While this is true in some cases, there is a lot more going on in our brains than we think.

In this chapter, we'll look at genetics' role in shaping personality and how our environment affects us throughout our lives. We'll also explore what happens when you combine both factors to create a unique individual—someone who may not fit neatly into any category or label.

What is Personality?

Even if we are familiar with the definition of personality provided by dictionaries, gaining a more profound comprehension of this idea will assist us in
28

developing a deeper appreciation for human psychology.

The term "personality" originates from the Latin word "persona," which refers to a theatrical mask used by players either to portray various characters or to hide their identity. Personality, according to psychologists, is defined as the pattern of ideas, emotions, and actions that distinguishes one person from another. It is believed that a person maintains these patterns throughout their whole life.

Before we go any further in this book, it is essential to properly understand the concept of personality since it serves as the foundation for this book.

There are a million different ways to define the concept of personality. However, for the sake of this book, let's consider the following definitions of personality.

Personality is the different patterns of conduct (including thoughts that affect feelings, emotions, and actions) that persistently define each individual and make up an individual's character.

It also refers to the distinctive thinking, feeling, and behavioral patterns unique to each individual and the psychological processes that underlie those patterns, whether hidden or not.

Personality may be defined as a pattern of generally stable features and distinctive qualities that provide a person's conduct with coherence and distinctiveness. These traits and characteristics make up a person's personality.

You can think of your personality as an expression of who you are, internally and externally. Your personality isn't just how you act or what you say—it's all those things combined with how other people perceive them.

While some people may view personality as something that can be changed, others believe it's inborn or predetermined. The truth is that while both of these ideas have merit, they are not mutually exclusive. Personality is developed through many factors, including both genetics and environment.

The study of personality primarily focuses on two distinct but interrelated areas. The first step is gaining an awareness of individual variances in certain personality traits, such as friendliness or impatience. The second component is understanding how the many aspects of a person contribute to the formation of the person as a whole.

How Do We Form Our Personalities?

Our personalities make us distinctive, but how do they develop? What aspects play the most significant role in creating a person's personality? How does personality work after it has been developed? Is it possible for personality to evolve? From the beginning, these topics have been mired in debate, especially in the field of psychology.

There are several theories that notable psychologists have come up with to explain how personality develops and how it impacts a person. A vast majority of professionals think that personality evolves. However, when you are born, you do not lack a personality—rather, it is in its most basic manifestation, known as temperament. Therefore, the lifelong learning experiences that shape your personality may be influenced by your temperament, comprised of natural characteristics such as energy levels, mood and attitude, and emotional receptivity. These phases of development start while we are young and play an essential part in determining who we will become as adults.

Here are five popular kinds of theories of personality formation:

- Trait Theories

Trait theories are grounded in biology. They make a distinction between characteristics and conditions. Personality is made up of solid and consistent features shown in most settings. These traits are what make up an individual's personality. Researchers can identify the connection between characteristics, thoughts, feelings, and behaviors.

- Psychodynamic Theories

Sigmund Freud's writings significantly impacted the development of psychodynamic theories, which emphasize the role that our unconscious mind plays in shaping our personalities. The subconscious mind is largely responsible for the patterns of both our thinking and our behavior. Theories such as Freud's Psychosexual Stage Theory and Erik Erikson's Stages of Psychosocial Development are examples of psychodynamic approaches to human development.

● Behavioral Theories

The belief held by behavioral theorists is that an individual's personality is formed by their interactions with their surroundings. However, these theories ignore the significance of an individual's interior thoughts and emotions, instead focusing on the individual's visible and quantifiable acts.

● Humanist Theories

Humanist theorists believe that an individual's free will is the primary factor that contributes to the formation of one's personality. It is considered that an individual's personality develops as they get older due to the ideas and activities they choose for themselves, in addition to the many experiences they have during their lifetime. This viewpoint is far more open to the many possibilities and factors that might contribute to the development of an individual's personality. Humanist thinkers include Carl Rogers and Abraham Maslow, among others.

● Social Cognitive Theory

This theory considers the unique way in which individuals acquire and maintain behavior while also considering the social environment in which individuals perform the behavior. The theory takes into account a person's past experiences, influences, and interactions—all of which shape whether a person will engage in a specific behavior and the reasons why a person engages in that behavior.

We're born with certain personality traits that make us unique, but our life experiences shape our personalities. We learn things from our environment, parents, friends, and teachers—and then we develop into adults with these traits ingrained in us. So even though we're not born with all this knowledge about how to interact with others or make decisions about how to live our lives, we learn from each experience as we go along until, eventually, those patterns become a part of who we are.

Genetics

Personality is formed by the interactions between your genes and your environment.

Genes are the basic building blocks of life, and they determine your physical characteristics, such as hair color and body shape. They also set limits on how tall you can grow, how fast your heart beats, and how easily you gain weight.

The environment also plays a role in forming personality. Your environment includes everything that has happened to you from birth until now—your relationships with family members and friends, experiences at school or work, recreational activities like sports or hobbies, and even the books you've read or movies you've watched.

The combination of genes and environment produces a unique personality. Some people are born with certain traits that make them more likely to develop certain personalities than others. For example, genetics may make it easier for some people to become outgoing, while others may be shy by nature but learn social skills through practice or training.

Components of Personality

You might be wondering what exactly makes up a person's personality. For a characteristic to be regarded as a component of an individual's personality, it must be shown repeatedly when confronted with circumstances that are analogous to one another. In other words, when a particular situation is presented to a person, the individual responds, in the same manner, every time with very few to no deviations.

Although one's personality is shaped mainly by thoughts and feelings, studies have shown that one's physical (biological) processes and requirements also play a role.

Personality isn't simply a matter of who we are on the inside—it also affects how we act and compels us to do certain actions. Personality may also be seen in the connections we form and how we portray ourselves to
36

the general public.

Furthermore, the components of a person's personality are defined by a model that suggests that human personality may be assessed across five broad personality qualities, known as The Big Five (OCEAN).

The Big Five theory proposes that all individuals, regardless of gender, age, or culture, have the same fundamental personality qualities but vary in the degree to which these traits are shown in their behavior. This indicates that the characteristics are rated on a scale that ranges from one thing to the opposite of that item and that we are free to place ourselves wherever we fit along that spectrum.

- **O**penness (Inventive - Curious vs. Consistent - Cautious)

Some people live for new experiences and aren't afraid to put themselves in dangerous situations, while others prefer to avoid danger and remain in their safe space. Openness relates to a person's willingness to participate in various life experiences. For example, a creative and curious person is likely to have more active cognitive processes and the ability to investigate various approaches to finding a solution to a particular issue. On the other hand, someone who is reliable and cautious is likely more at ease adhering to the prescribed procedures and regulations.

- **C**onscientiousness (Efficient - Organized vs. Easy-going - Carefree)

The level of conscientiousness can gauge the degree of spontaneity an individual possesses. Effective and well-organized people value the feeling of having control over their environment. Consequently, they tend toward perfectionism, begin planning everything from the first day, and feel compelled to adhere to a predetermined structure. On the other hand, people who are carefree and easygoing do not focus as much on the process itself so long as the task at hand is completed successfully. They look at things from a high-level perspective rather than focusing on the minute particulars of the situation.

- **E**xtroversion (Outgoing - Energetic vs. Solitary - Reserved)

You must be familiar with the dichotomy between

38

extroverts and introverts. Extroversion is the capacity and enthusiasm of an individual to participate in social interactions with others. It's about being sociable, having a lot of energy, and being friendly. Extroverts are more outgoing than introverts and often make choices on the spur of the moment. These individuals sometimes engage in risky behavior without carefully considering the repercussions of their actions. On the other hand, introverts prefer to work alone or with just a small group of carefully chosen colleagues. This is because they have an internal focus, as they dislike being the center of attention for others.

- **A**greeableness (Friendly - Compassionate vs. Cold - Unkind)

To get along with others, you must demonstrate an open mind and sympathy. You must be pleasant to converse with and a good team player. People often feel that you are agreeable and simple to collaborate with. On the other hand, someone uncaring and self-absorbed may be described as having a frigid disposition. It's possible that this individual does not have empathy and has no idea how to care properly for those around them. There is no denying the fact that this quality might make it challenging to develop connections with other individuals.

- **Neuroticism (Sensitive - Nervous vs. Secure - Confident)**

Neuroticism refers to a person's emotional steadiness and adaptability to various circumstances, e.g., stress. Very emotional and sensitive people are considerably more likely to buckle under pressure. They often struggle with difficulties of confidence and low self-esteem at their core. However, the circumstances around them don't readily shake those who are confident in themselves. They have a solid emotional basis and a strong sense of who they are, which allows them to make sound choices even when the stakes are high.

Can Personality Evolve?

In the past, psychologists fought about whether or not personality is a function of socialization or biology (this refers to the never-ending nature vs. nurture debate). As the study has advanced, they have become more confident that the two are not incompatible with one another. Both genes and surroundings influence one's personality. While genetics are absolute, the environment is mutable.

This is one of the reasons why psychologists such as Carol Dweck feel that some characteristics of one's personality may be altered to some extent. These characteristics are what she refers to as the "in-between" characteristics. Some examples of these in-between characteristics are belief systems, objectives, and coping mechanisms. These are the features discovered on top of your established attributes—they are dependable, unchangeable characteristics.

Changing your belief system (for example, your philosophy or religion) can significantly impact your general way of thinking and feeling. The same is true for a person's life objectives and the methods they use to deal with stress. When someone makes these adjustments, their mind and body will eventually catch up to the changes. As a result of this, they experience a change in their personality.

Earlier in this chapter, we spoke about how personality

does not change throughout one's life. However, some characteristics can be modified because of the continuously shifting environment.

Is it possible for a person to modify the unfavorable aspects of their personality? How?

The transition from one personality type to another may seem impossible, but in reality, it is possible, at least to some degree.

Changing your routines should be your primary emphasis to alter a personality type. As a result of the fact that habits are acquired via training, changing your behavior in small ways over time may significantly influence your personality and move it in a more positive direction. This covers your typical reactions, coping techniques, and tactics for dealing with difficult situations.

Keep your attention on the procedure. Recognize the value of your efforts, but do not allow yourself to become disheartened if some of your talents slow down the process. Be conscious of the areas in which you might improve.

Finally, pay attention to how you can improve. Always keep in mind that developing yourself is a trip that is always worth taking, no matter how challenging it may be. If you want to alter your personality for the better, you need to differentiate the in-between qualities from the fixed ones you were born with and figure out how you can improve the in-between features.

Can Personality Be Shaped?

A person's personality is shaped by their genetic makeup, experiences, and environment. While inborn traits and characteristics help shape how people respond to their experiences, their environment also shapes how personality is formed and expressed. People are born with a dominant personality type that environmental factors and experiences can then shape. This means that certain traits are more likely to manifest themselves in some individuals than others, depending on how they were raised and what experiences they had growing up.

43

While genetics play an essential role in shaping our personalities, we must note that we can also change our behavior by changing our thoughts or environment.

The way we see ourselves is called self-concept, and it's made up of three parts:

1) **Self-esteem** is our overall opinion of ourselves or how we feel about ourselves.

2) **Self-perception** is how we view ourselves and our place in the world.

3) **Self-image** is what we think other people see when they look at us, which can be different from how we perceive ourselves.

We develop our self-concepts as children by observing our parents' behavior and how they treat us. The way they respond to us influences how we think about ourselves later on in life, so if your parents were always negative toward you or didn't express any love for you, then chances are your self-esteem will be low, and

44

you'll have trouble believing that anyone else can love you either.

Understanding Your Personality Type

Step 1: Determining Your Personality Type

Determining your personality type can help you learn more about your motivations and how you interact and relate to others.

Understanding your personality type can be useful for self-improvement, as you can better understand how to interact with others. It can also help you understand why you act the way you do in certain situations, allowing for better decision-making in the future.

It is important to remember that there are no right answers when determining your personality type—rather, there are simply different ways of thinking about yourself and others. There is no one "right" way of doing things.

What is your personality type?

Although there are many personality tests, the most

common is based on the Myers-Briggs Type Indicator (MBTI), developed by Katharine Cook Briggs and her daughter Isabel Briggs-Myers. The MBTI categorizes people into one of 16 different types based on their preferences for interacting with the world around them.

The first step in determining your personality type is taking a free online test to help determine your preferences. You can then use this information to better understand yourself and how you interact with other people and how they perceive you.

The MBTI measures four different categories:

1) Extraversion vs. Introversion—Do you gain energy from being around other people or alone?

2) Sensing vs. Intuition—Do you prefer facts or abstractions? (Usually, this means concrete facts vs. abstract ideas.)

3) Thinking vs. Feeling—Do you make decisions based on logic or emotions?

4) Judging vs. Perceiving—Do you like structure and order or spontaneity and flexibility?

Step 2: Understanding Cognitive distortions

To understand your personality, you must also understand the concept of cognitive distortions. Cognitive distortions are irrational thoughts and beliefs that we have about ourselves, others, and the world around us. These distortions can cause us to feel negative emotions like anger, sadness, or shame. Cognitive distortions can also be responsible for some of our less-than-ideal behaviors, such as overeating or turning to alcohol to numb our pain.

Often, these distortions are so ingrained in our thinking that we don't even realize they're happening. We may think things like, "I'm always late," or "I'm not good enough," without realizing that these thoughts aren't actually true. These distortions can lead to anxiety, depression, and other mental health issues if left unchecked.

Cognitive distortions lead us to believe that we are not good enough, that everyone else is better than us, or that the world is out to get us. They also cause us to believe that we are in control when the opposite is true. These distorted thoughts are irrational because they don't match up with reality.

Cognitive distortions can be positive or negative, but they primarily tend to be negative because they make things seem worse than they are.

Here are a few examples of cognitive distortions:

- **All or Nothing Thinking**

This thought process involves only seeing things in black-and-white terms—there is no middle ground between two extremes (e.g., "If I don't finish this project perfectly today, then it's not worth doing at all").

- **Overgeneralization**

This thought process involves generalizing from one bad experience and applying it to other situations (e.g., "I failed my driving test today, so now I'll never get my license"). This involves making broad generalizations about yourself or others based on one negative event

48

or situation. For example, if someone cancels plans with you because of a headache, this might trigger thoughts such as, "They didn't really want to hang with me," or "People always let me down."

- **Mental Filter**

This involves paying attention only to certain details while ignoring others—often resulting in negative conclusions. For example, if someone forgets your birthday and buys you a gift later that month, this could trigger focusing exclusively on the negative in your life while ignoring the positive.

- **Disqualifying the Positive**

Someone disqualifying the positive will reject positive experiences by insisting they "don't count" for some reason or another.

- **Jumping to Conclusions**

This cognitive distortion leads us to assume we know what will happen even when there is no evidence to support our belief, such as believing others have negative opinions about us without checking first.

- **Mind Reading**

This refers to believing we know what other people are thinking about us without asking them or having any evidence.

Step 3: Understanding the Link Between Habits and Personality

But there's a lot more to it than that! People are also creatures of personality, which means they have certain tendencies, preferences, and reactions—things they repeatedly do. And most of the time, those things are habits.

For example: if you're someone who gets up early every morning because your alarm goes off at 6 AM every day, that's a habit. You don't have to think about it—you just turn off your alarm and roll out of bed. But if you like eating peanut butter sandwiches for lunch every day because it reminds you of when you were little, that's not just a habit—that's also part of your personality (and probably one of your favorite parts).

The more we do something, the more ingrained it becomes in our behavior. When we have good habits

50

and behaviors, they can help us achieve our goals and dreams. But sometimes, our habits can hold us back from achieving the things we want most.

When you start a new job, you might find yourself doing things that aren't aligned with your core values or beliefs—but that's okay! It's natural to start out by just doing what you're told. Suppose you want to succeed at something new or different than what you've done before. In that case, it's essential to really think about whether your current habits are helping or hurting you.

The way we think, act, and make decisions is largely based on our habits. Our brains are wired to be habitual—it's how we learn new things, decide what to do next, and even remember things from our past. Habits are your brain's operating system—you can go through life automatically without even realizing it!

People are creatures of habit. We have a certain way we like to do things, and it can be challenging if you're trying to change that habit. But as much as we tend to stick with what's comfortable, there are things in life that we just need to learn how to do differently—and one of those things is learning how to make healthy changes in our lives.

Step 4: Understanding Self-Awareness

Self-awareness is vital to being a well-rounded, emotionally healthy person. Self-awareness gives us insight into our emotional health and helps us understand why we respond the way we do. When we're aware of ourselves and our emotions, we can overcome unhealthy patterns that influence poor decision-making and relational strains.

Self-awareness is the ability to understand and acknowledge your thoughts, feelings, and behaviors. It's a skill that can help you better understand why you respond the way you do—and how to change those responses for the better.

As we grow in self-awareness, we learn how our past experiences shape who we are and how those experiences influence our current emotions and reactions. The more aware of your patterns, the easier it is to change unhealthy habits that negatively affect your decisions or your relationships.

Chapter 2: The Enneagram

If you've ever wondered why you're always stressed, why you can't seem to get along with your boss, or why that one friend of yours drives you crazy, this might be the section for you. The Enneagram is one of the most powerful tools to promote self-reflection and personal growth.

It's a system of nine personality types that helps us understand how we interact with others, what motivates us, and what makes us tick. It offers an incredible amount of insight into who we are as individuals and how we relate to others around us.

<u>What Is the Enneagram?</u>

The word *Enneagram* stems from the Greek language—*ennea* meaning "nine" and *gram* meaning "drawing" or "diagram." The Enneagram is a geometric figure that maps out the nine fundamental personality types of human nature and their complex interrelationships. The concept of the modern-day Enneagram system is credited to Bolivian philosopher Oscar Ichazo, who in 1968 created the Arica Institute, a school that taught consciousness methodologies, including the Enneagram. Pioneering Chilean psychiatrist Claudio Naranjo came to Arica to learn more and instantly became interested in the Enneagram as a result of his own journey of self-discovery. He would go on to create the Seekers After Truth Institute, an international training program in which the Enneagram plays a central role.

The concept of the Enneagram has grown and is now taught worldwide at accredited schools operated through the International Enneagram Association. Psychologists and mental health therapists are beginning to use the Enneagram in their practices to help individuals recognize their motivations and how they may be holding them back.

The Enneagram is more than a personality test. It's a typing system (meaning it establishes "types") designed to understand our motivations. Enneagram experts will quickly tell students that this methodology is not an excuse to engage in certain behaviors just because they may be typical of a certain type. The Enneagram consists of nine different types, each representing a different core motivation and core fears that each drive the decisions you make, whether you're aware of it or not. The nine types represent nine ways of viewing the world. Enneagram theory maintains that everyone has a core fear and a core desire that make up their Enneagram type. This means that each person's core fear and desire determine how they will act, respond, and interact with the world.

The Enneagram focuses on Why Over What. This crucial distinction differentiates it from other personality tests - Instead of focusing on **WHAT** you do, the Enneagram focuses on **WHY** you do what you do. It's a system that can help you understand your personality type and how it affects your relationships and interactions with others. It's also helpful in understanding how you respond to stress, personally and professionally, and how you handle criticism or setbacks in your life.

The Enneagram is a prominent personality diagnostic instrument that fosters self-awareness, empathy, and personal development. It has nine main archetypes, or personality types, each assigned a specific number. The physical representation of the Enneagram as a geometric shape has these numerical values charted at various points (see figure below). The connections among these symbolic numbers correspond to the behaviors demonstrated by each represented type. Each Enneagram personality type, or enneatype, is a description of an individual's primary motivating force or inner emotional drive rather than a characterization of their outward appearance or role in any social group.

The Enneagram helps you develop compassion for yourself and others. It allows you to see some of the most challenging parts of yourself that you can't see without intentional reflection. It gives you a blueprint for understanding why you act the way you do. And if you can do the hard work and look at those blueprints, you will finally have what you need to begin growing in a long-lasting, transformative way.

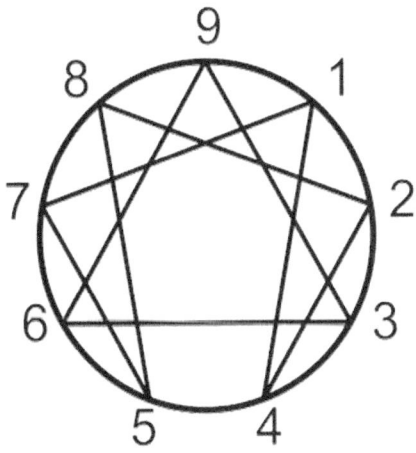

Each number around the circle represents one of these nine personality types:

1) The Perfectionist
2) The Helper

3) The Achiever
4) The Individualist
5) The Investigator
6) The Loyalist
7) The Enthusiast
8) The Challenger
9) The Peacemaker

The test is used to evaluate people and their personalities. Still, it's not meant to be definitive or permanent—it's simply intended as a starting point for self-reflection and personal growth. The Enneagram can help you better understand yourself and others, but it's not meant to be used as an excuse or explanation for poor behavior.

The Enneagram does not evaluate you based on how others perceive you or how you interact with them—it is primarily based upon self-reported evidence, which is why it cannot claim to be a technical or scientific method. Enneagram evaluation heavily focuses on self-awareness rather than externally imposed measurement and analyses, making this method so effective for many people. It may take longer to identify our own types than it would for others to judge and convey their impressions to us in the name of guidance, but the journey to find oneself can be healing and rewarding, as well as character-building. Furthermore, when we can see ourselves in more than just one of the archetype descriptions, we subconsciously work to enhance our empathetic capacities by considering the world from varying vantage points.

It may help to think of the enneatypes not as different personalities but as different forms of modus operandi. They do not accurately predict what colors or flavors we'll enjoy most, or what genres of music and literature will spark our interests; they don't always determine the degrees of introversion or extroversion that we display; they cannot always explain the types of careers, lifestyles, and lovers that we choose. Instead, the enneatypes describe road maps, blueprints, or operating systems. They plot out the varied ways in which people interact with the world based on differing perspectives. The Enneagram focuses on the motivations behind our actions and how these motivations are often defined early in life by experiences that teach us what our role in life should be, or how best to survive in the face of risk and uncertainty.

What Can the Enneagram Offer You?

The Enneagram is a tool that helps you to understand yourself, your relationships, and the world around you. It can help you:

- Understand how your mind works.
- Identify patterns in your behavior.
- See how these behavioral patterns affect your relationships with others.

Understand your personality

The Enneagram can offer a way to understand yourself and the people around you. The Enneagram is a system that organizes personalities into nine types, each with unique strengths and challenges. By learning about your type, you'll better understand yourself and how you interact with the people around you. It's one of the most effective tools for identifying your deepest motivations, and it can help you discover how those motivations play out in your life and relationships.

The Enneagram types are not made up of lists of character traits, but are founded on a person's core values. Each type represents a fundamental decision about what is most important in life, such as power, security, harmony, knowledge, or fulfillment. This decision is a two-edged sword - focusing on any of these essential values enables us to make a valuable contribution in many areas of life. Still, it also causes us to neglect other values, creating a psychological 'blind spot' that limits our perspective and prevents us from developing beyond a certain point.

Identifying your Enneagram type can show you this blind spot and open up unexpected options for change. It can help you break long-standing patterns that have been holding you back, sometimes without your realizing it.

Discover your gifts, talents, and blind spots.

The Enneagram is a powerful tool for personal growth. It can help you understand the patterns of your thinking and behavior, which will help you understand why you do what you do, and how those patterns affect your relationships with others. It can also help you identify critical areas of your life where you may need to make changes in order to achieve your goals and be happier.

The Enneagram is a personality system that allows you to understand yourself and others more deeply. It gives you a language to describe your strengths, weaknesses, and motivations. It also helps you identify where people of other "types" might have different strengths and weaknesses so that you can work together more effectively.

Increase emotional intelligence

The Enneagram is a great way to learn to be more compassionate and empathetic toward others and ourselves. It's also extremely useful for helping us understand why we do the things we do and how we can change our behavior for the better. The Enneagram offers you a way to understand yourself, your motivations, and the choices you make. It helps you understand why you make your choices and their impact on those around you.

In addition to being an effective tool for self-discovery, many believe the Enneagram can help us better understand others. It's sometimes used in therapy settings and by business leaders and people who want to improve their interpersonal relationships. Understanding your own and others' Enneagram types allows you to relate to others with greater empathy and compassion, leading to less conflict and more transparent communication.

Professional development

Whether or not knowing your strengths and weaknesses is important to you personally, it is vital to your professional development. Without this knowledge, you risk choosing the wrong challenges or even the wrong career. You are also likely to keep coming up against the same obstacles to success.

Identifying and working with your Enneagram type can help you play to your strengths by choosing goals that are most appealing and appropriate for your talents. Knowing your 'blind spot' helps you work around the obstacles it creates for you.

It's hard to think of a job in which dealing with people is not a vital skill. For anyone in one of the 'people professions' - such as managing, teaching, counseling, coaching, consulting, sales, medicine, or politics - it is central to the success or failure of your work.

The Enneagram offers a robust framework for relating to others more authentically and constructively. Whether influencing, managing, selling, caring, team-building, presenting, or advising, it can help you communicate effectively and respectfully, extending your influence and opening up new options for collaboration.

Uses of the Enneagram

It's important to emphasize that your Enneagram type is determined by what motivates you to do what you do. The levels of development consist of specific behaviors that correspond to each type. When an Enneagram type is in a good place, they are considered "healthy." When healthy, the person feels like they are free to express themselves through wide ranges of behavior. Most people fall under the "average" level of development, which is when we are in a neutral place. Here we focus more on our own identity and how others view us. When we're not at our best, we are at the "unhealthy" level of development. During these times, we tend to see ourselves differently than how others see us. We are not in tune with our identity at all.

The descriptions of healthy versus unhealthy behaviors differ from those associated with the stress versus security lines. When the Enneagram system refers to the stress line, these are behaviors that Enneagram types tend to take on when they are experiencing periods of stress. For example, an Enneagram Type Two might snap into aggressive behavior when experiencing stress, which is typically more characteristic of an Enneagram Type Eight. They might be considered a "healthy" Two, but one stressful moment led them to access their stress line. Security appears differently, and it is also situational, like when we are having a happy moment or positive experience in a good place or feeling secure in who we are. We can be a healthy version of our type, while not being in a situation of security or growth.

In addition to being useful for personal growth and understanding, the Enneagram can also be used to help understand group dynamics and organizational structures. For example, suppose an organization has several teams working together on a project. In that case, this test can help identify which team members are most likely to clash or collaborate effectively and suggest how the leaders might manage those dynamics accordingly.

Professional use—helping managers and leaders better understand their employees' strengths, weaknesses, communication styles, etc.

Personal use—helping to identify your type so you can work on your weaknesses and find ways to improve your communication skills.

Here are some additional ways you can use the Enneagram:

- Learn about your strengths and weaknesses. The Enneagram has been used for centuries to help people better understand themselves and others and their relationships with each other. The insights gained from this practice can be used to improve relationships and find balance in life.
- Identify which type your friends and family members are so you can appreciate them for who they are.
- By understanding their type, discover what motivates others to work with you or against you.
- Understand how you react to different situations in your life and why you react that way.
- Understand why other people act the way they do in certain situations.
- Experience personal growth by recognizing patterns of behavior that may be holding you back from reaching your full potential.

- Increase emotional intelligence

The Enneagram and Self Awareness

When thinking about oneself and one's actions, it is essential to have both self-awareness and mindfulness of those actions. You must first become aware that something is taking place before you can accept and admit the possibility that you have a propensity to respond to certain circumstances in a particular manner.

The Enneagram is one of the most powerful tools to help us develop self-awareness and become the highest expression of ourselves. It is a personality assessment that can help you identify your personality type and understand why you act the way you do in certain situations. It can also help you understand others better so that you can be more effective in your interactions with them.

Millions of people worldwide have used the Enneagram to help them understand themselves, their relationships, and their work lives. The Enneagram helps us see ourselves as human beings who are

70

constantly growing and evolving and allows us to see how our past experiences continue to influence our present choices.

We all have different personalities but share specific characteristics that make us similar. These similarities allow us to relate to each other more deeply. The Enneagram shows us how we all have something unique to offer each other as we learn from each other's strengths and weaknesses to grow together as individuals committed to improving ourselves for the good of humanity.

Self-awareness is an integral part of emotional intelligence. It gives you insight into your emotional health and why you respond the way you do. Self-awareness also helps you grow self-confidence, an essential skill for making good decisions and building healthy relationships.

Self-awareness is crucial to your success. Self-awareness allows you to be honest with yourself about what you're capable of and what challenges you may face. When you understand yourself and your strengths, you can take advantage of them. You can also use that knowledge to identify areas where you might need to develop more skills.

- **Self-awareness is a tool to help you to understand yourself better**

Self-awareness is also helpful in relationships with others. If you know how to recognize your feelings and reactions, then it's easier for you to understand what's happening in the minds of those around you. This makes it easier for both parties to communicate effectively and avoid misunderstandings or hurt feelings on either side.

- **Self-awareness makes you more effective in your relationships**

Self-awareness is a skill that can make you more effective in your personal and work relationships and all areas of your life. Self-awareness is the ability to see yourself as others see you. It helps you understand how you come across to other people, how your actions and words affect others, and how others perceive your motives. When you're self-aware, you're better able to identify what's important to you so that you can set goals and make decisions that align with those values.

- **Self-awareness helps you recognize when something isn't right**

Being self-aware means knowing yourself well enough that you're able to make informed choices about what matters most in life. It also means recognizing when something isn't right in your life—such as a bad relationship—and taking action to improve things for yourself.

- **Self-awareness leads to better decision making**

Self-awareness is the ability to recognize your strengths, weaknesses, and emotions. It's essential to be self-aware because it helps you understand yourself better and make decisions that are right for you. When you're self-aware, you can be confident in who you are as an individual. That means that when you have to decide on something that might not be easy, like choosing between two jobs or deciding whether or not to break up with someone, your confidence will help guide you through those tough choices.

- **Being self-aware also means recognizing your own emotions**

For instance, if you're feeling scared about making a big decision in life or if someone has done something mean to you, identifying the emotion you're feeling will help clarify what's going on and how best to handle it.

Self-awareness is one of the most important things you can have in your life. It allows you to understand who you are, what you want, and how to get it. Without it, you can end up living a life that doesn't really fit who you are or a life that's not very fulfilling to you.

When you're self-aware, you understand how your emotions affect your decisions and relationships. This gives you the power to break unhealthy patterns and make better decisions.

Self-awareness is a process that helps you identify the underlying causes of your feelings and behaviors so that you can overcome them. It's not meant to be a quick fix or an easy way out—self-awareness is a lifelong journey that requires commitment and dedication from both yourself and those who care about you.

The Enneagram can help you become more self-aware by providing a list of typical characteristics and behaviors of each type. It contains components from ancient systems that have been around for thousands of years. In the twentieth century, it was developed into the personality system we know today by observing people and their behaviors to understand what drives them. The Enneagram can be used for personal growth, as well as for helping others to grow.

Overview of the Enneagram Types

The Enneagram has nine different personality types. Each type contains a unique combination of characteristics that make up its overall identity. Each type also has its strengths and weaknesses, which means people of each type must understand their own type's tendencies so they can work on those areas where improvement is needed.

You'll want to find out what type you are because it will help you understand why you react in certain ways when faced with certain situations or people. For example, if someone from another personality type does something that bothers you, knowing what type they are will help you understand why this person might have done that—and whether or not there is anything else going on that might be causing them to act the way they do.

Here is the basic overview of the nine personality types. The names of the Enneagram types given here are not definitive - different teachers use different names, and some just refer to the types by number.

Type 1: Perfectionist

Perfectionists are responsible, organized, and conscientious. They want things to be as close to perfect as possible, and they're willing to put in the work to make that happen. Keep on learning and improving, and keep doing what makes YOU happy. While you may sometimes feel like your standards are too high, it's important to remember that it's not about the result but the journey.

When you're a Perfectionist, it can be hard to relax.

You want everything to be just so, and you don't mind spending hours on something if it means you can perfect it. It's all about the craftsmanship, and that's what drives you. But sometimes, taking a break from your craft can help you get back into the zone. A little time away from the project might clarify what needs fixing and how to fix it. So take some time off!

Type 2: The Helper

If you have this personality type, you are known for your ability to connect with others, your enthusiasm for helping others succeed, and your desire to make the world a better place. You are also known for being empathetic and understanding of other people's feelings, which makes you a great listener and a supportive friend.

The Helper is someone who cares deeply about the well-being of others. You're very generous and kind and strongly desire to make your loved ones happy. You might enjoy helping people but have difficulty saying no when someone asks you for help.

You are excellent at listening and can be trusted with

confidential information. You tend to be very empathetic and often use your intuition to guide you in situations where logic would fail you. As a Helper, you tend to have difficulty caring for yourself because you focus so much on caring for others. You might feel like a failure when things go wrong in your life or when you cannot help someone else with something important to them (e.g., an illness, death, etc.).

Type 3: The Achiever

The Achiever is focused on success. You're motivated, ambitious, competitive, and driven to accomplish your goals. You enjoy being valuable and able to get the job done. You like to win and hate to lose. You want to be the best in your field, and you often are. You know yourself well and are usually able to manage your life effectively. While you can be impatient with others, you typically have the patience necessary to get things done. Your greatest strengths include your ability to take action, focus on the results rather than the process, and let go of things that aren't working. At times you might become too focused on achieving results at all costs.

Type 4: The Individualist

As an Individualist, you are highly creative and constantly attempting to express your individuality. Your focus lies in maintaining your individuality and uniqueness and presenting yourself authentically and transparently. You are self-aware, expressive, romantic, and true to yourself. You might also be deeply sensitive and emotional.

Type 5: The Investigator

The Investigator is all about the facts. You are focused on gaining an understanding of things and providing insight to others. You are knowledgeable, innovative, and extremely private. You love solving problems and figuring out how things work—and, more importantly, why they work. You're great at coming up with logical solutions for complex problems.

You have a lot of knowledge on a wide range of topics and like sharing your wisdom with others. You enjoy reading a lot and learning new things about history or science.

Type 6: The Loyalist

The Loyalist is focused on security. You desire to maintain a level of comfort that feels right for you. You are reliable, trustworthy, devoted, and committed to everything around you. You are a true friend and will stick by anyone who has earned your trust. You're always there for people who need help or support, but you also know when to give them space. People love being around you because they know you'll never abandon or turn against them.

Type 7: The Enthusiast

The Enthusiast is energetic, enthusiastic, and expressive. Your focus lies in experiencing as many things as possible and living life to the fullest. You love to be around people and always look for ways to make them happy. You are great at helping others feel comfortable in social situations and enjoy being the life of the party.

Type 8: The Challenger

The Challenger is honest, assertive, independent, and happy to take charge. As a Challenger, you're a natural-born leader who doesn't lead by example—you lead through inspiration and through challenging others to reach their potential. Type Eights are often highly competitive and ambitious. You might be ruthless when it comes to getting what you want and making sure you're the best at what you do, but you typically only do this because you genuinely want to help those around you grow and succeed.

Challengers aren't afraid to ask for help when they need it—and they're also not afraid to ask for forgiveness when they've made a mistake. You know that no one's perfect and that being human means making mistakes sometimes. But this doesn't stop you from being driven toward success at all costs.

Type 9: The Peacemaker

The Peacemaker is easygoing, adaptable, understanding, and supportive. You focus on maintaining a peaceful environment for yourself and the people around you. As a Peacemaker, you do not like conflict and seek to avoid it. You are very sensitive and empathetic. You tend to be very compassionate, kind, and generous. You might have a strong sense of

81

morality and integrity, but if you feel that someone has wronged you, you will hold grudges for a long time.

You are usually calm and easy-going, so you can get along with everyone. You don't like confrontation or drama, so you'll do your best not to create it. You enjoy helping others and may be drawn to humanitarian work or helping needy communities. You may also be interested in working with animals or environmental conservation. As a Peacemaker, you are happiest when you have the freedom to work at your own pace and do not need to be micromanaged or given specific goals and deadlines. Your primary goal is ensuring everyone around you feels safe and secure.

Potential Pitfalls of the Enneagram

The Enneagram is a powerful tool for self-discovery. It can help you understand yourself and others better and guide you toward your life's purpose. But it does have its pitfalls. Here are some things to keep in mind if you're using the Enneagram for self-reflection or development.

1) The Enneagram is not a magic tool. If you're looking for something that will magically fix all of your problems, the Enneagram is not it. You must be prepared to put in the effort and do the work of self-development to see results. You also need to be ready for setbacks along the way (which are inevitable).

2) Your number does NOT define you. It shows you the defense mechanisms you most readily and subconsciously go to in life.

3) Don't limit yourself. The Enneagram isn't meant to label people or put them into boxes—it's simply a framework for better understanding yourself and others. It's a tool that can help you navigate relationships more effectively and find fulfillment in life, but don't let it become an obsession!

4) It's easy to become obsessed with your type, even if you're unsure which one it is.

5) You might want to try out every type because they sound cool or different.

6) It's important to remember that no types are better or worse than the others. Each type has

strengths and weaknesses, opportunities and obstacles.

7) You can use this information as an excuse for behavior that isn't helpful—like saying, "I'm an Eight," when someone asks why you yelled at them.

8) The Enneagram is a tool to get to know yourself and others better, but it can also be used to judge, compare, and criticize. It can be tempting to look at the different personality types to find some are more similar than others. But this creates an unnecessary divide between people and their personalities—and it's not healthy.

9) We all have the potential to occupy any position on the Enneagram, and in different situations, we can take on the characteristics of any of the nine types.

10) Finding your number can be a lengthy discovery process for some people. Don't be discouraged.

11) Once you find your number, you may not be happy about it. This is because your subconscious starts to get uncomfortable when you identify the unconscious motivations behind your number.

12) Knowing your number is not the end. It's the beginning of your growth journey with the Enneagram.

The Enneagram is a powerful tool for self-discovery. However, it's important to remember that this isn't a perfect system. Some psychologists have criticized the Enneagram for its lack of scientific validity. It's important to remember that while the Enneagram gives us a lot of information about our personal patterns and tendencies, it doesn't tell us everything about ourselves—and it doesn't tell us everything about other people.

CHAPTER 3: THE NINE ENNEAGRAM TYPES

Type One: The Perfectionist

Traits

Ethical and conscientious, Perfectionists tend to feel a strong need to improve themselves and others. They have a set of ideals and values that are important to them, and they want people to do the right thing. They're known for being organized, creating order, and maintaining high standards for themselves and others. They might have problems with resentment and being critical of others if they do things differently. At their best, they are inspiring, wise, and moral. They want to be good, have integrity, and be balanced. Fairness is important to them. They fear being seen as a bad person, corrupt, or wrong.

Beliefs

Dissatisfied with the status quo, Perfectionists feel it is up to them to improve everything. They are motivated by the need to live their life the right way, including improving themselves and the world around them. Afraid of making mistakes, they desire everything to be consistent with their ideals. They are impatient and never satisfied unless things are done "properly." Type Ones are also quite conscientious, so they are likely to be organized and orderly in their lives. They believe in setting goals, planning ahead, and doing things logically.

Strengths

Type Ones are the people who never stop learning. They're constantly refining their skills, taking on new challenges, and learning more about the world around them. They're always ready to improve and want others to improve their lives too. They can see what is
88

wrong in any given situation and how to fix it.

Weaknesses

When it comes to working, Perfectionists prefer to tackle projects one at a time rather than taking on several at once. Because of their tendency toward being analytical and detached from their feelings, this personality type may also be prone to depression if they cannot live up to their expectations. Perfectionists become obsessed with the 'right way' to do things and refuse to give themselves or anyone else any peace until conformity is achieved.

Desires

Type Ones love to help others improve, whether it's through feedback or through sharing their knowledge with others. They're often interested in business and being a part of something bigger than themselves—but they value personal growth above all else.

Fears

Perfectionists are sensitive to criticism, but they often ignore it because they don't want to deal with their feelings about it. They get upset when things don't go how they want or expect them to. They can be stubborn and unwilling to compromise. They fear being labeled as bad, defective, evil, or corrupt.

Work and Career

Perfectionists tend to have a lot of goals and dreams. They might be ambitious and driven and probably have high standards for themselves (and the people around them). Perfectionists are efficient, organized, and always complete the task. The more analytical and tough-minded Ones are found in management, science, and law enforcement. The more people-oriented Ones are found in health care, education, and religious work. Since they do things professionally, honestly, and ethically, you would do well to have Ones as your car mechanic, surgeon, dentist, banker, and stockbroker.

Leadership Style

Perfectionists can be good leaders because they are confident in their abilities and know what they're doing, but they need help recognizing when someone else has a better solution than theirs.

Parenting Style

The Perfectionist parenting style focuses on being the best parent possible. This means they push their children to succeed and work hard in everything they do. The Perfectionist parenting style can be tough on children because it requires them to always perform at a high level. However, it does have its benefits as well. This parenting style can teach children how to focus on their goals and reach those goals through hard work and dedication.

Relationships

Perfectionists are loyal, dedicated, conscientious, and helpful at their best in relationships. They are well-balanced and have a good sense of humor. They are critical, argumentative, nit-picking and uncompromising at their worst. They have high expectations of others. Perfectionists want to control every aspect of their spouse's life and career. They expect perfection from their partner, and they can become frustrated and angry when they don't get it.

What Perfectionists do in stress

Perfectionists are naturally predisposed to stress. Type Ones care about quality and excellence, and they'll be more likely to feel overwhelmed when their work isn't up to standard. The best way to reduce stress as a Perfectionist is to change your mindset. Instead of thinking about the end result or how others will perceive your work (which is bound to cause stress), focus on the process. Think about what's going well and what needs improvement—and then try again!

What Perfectionists do in Peace

Perfectionists always strive for the best outcome. When they achieve it, they feel great! They want to make sure everyone else is okay. They want to ensure everyone else is happy, so they'll go out of their way to meet everyone else's needs. If someone is upset or sad, a perfectionist will try to comfort them and help them feel better.

Type Two: The Helper

Traits

Warmhearted and focused on relationships, the Helper tends to discount their own needs and feelings to serve others. They want people to feel loved and wanted, and they might have problems with people-pleasing and trouble saying "no." At their best, they are patient, generous, and forgiving. They want to be loved, wanted, needed and appreciated for their good deeds and what they do for others. They fear being unworthy of love and care from others. Generous to a fault, they can be relied on to step forward and care for others when needed. Their giving can take many forms - time, attention, energy, experience, influence, or money. They strive to improve others' lives by always being there for them. It's important to them to be liked and accepted by others and to alleviate the world of its problems. Typical behaviors of a Helper include:

- Being a mediator or conflict resolver.
- Being empathetic and sympathetic toward others' circumstances.

- Being a good listener who can provide advice when asked for it.

Beliefs

Helpers love to take care of people and are known for having a kind heart. These people are often natural caregivers who enjoy looking after others and ensuring they're happy. They also tend to be very affectionate, kind, and considerate people who are good at recognizing the needs of others. They're always ready to lend a hand. They might be excellent listeners but also know when it's time for action. Helping others gives them a sense of purpose. They feel like they instinctively know what other people need from them and know how others are feeling. They wish other people knew what they needed instead of having to tell them because they feel like it would show that they care.

Strengths

People with Type Two personalities are generally friendly and empathetic. They often focus on the needs of others, and they can be very good at meeting those needs. They enjoy helping others and may appear to be selfless. Twos understand the joy of service. They are happy to give without seeking a reward in return since making a difference in another's life is what pleases them. They find fulfillment in the act of giving.

Weaknesses

Helpers can feel guilty if they don't meet someone else's needs or if someone is upset with them. Type Two people can be quite sensitive to criticism or blame from others because they are so selfless.

Fears

If someone is upset with a Helper, the Helper may feel it's their fault because they want everyone around them to feel happy and loved. However, there is a fine line between being selfless and being codependent—type Twos need to remember that no one will take care of them if they don't take care of themselves first. They fear being unloved and unwanted.

Desires

Helpers have a fundamental desire to feel loved. They also tend to have an innate ability to help others heal emotionally through their words and actions. For example, they might be able to calm down someone with a panic attack or give advice on how best to deal with an argument between two friends without saying anything directly about what's going on between those friends (they just listen).

Work and Career

Helpers are often drawn toward careers where they can use their skills to help people achieve their goals, such as counselors, teachers, and health workers. They may also be drawn toward careers that allow them to work with children or animals because they love being around those who need support and encouragement. Helpers work in sales and help others as receptionists, secretaries, assistants, decorators, and consultants.

Leadership Style

The Helper is a natural leader. They are compassionate and empathetic, which makes them great at listening to their team members and helping them solve problems. The Helper's ability to listen and empathize also makes them good at managing other people's emotions, which means they can be a great mediator

96

when things get heated.

As a leader their leadership style is democratic. They don't like micromanaging or being micromanaged—they want everyone on their team to feel empowered! Helpers encourage everyone's input and make decisions based on what will work best for the team.

Parenting Style

The Helper is the parent overly concerned with their child's well-being and will often go out of their way to help their child succeed in all areas of life. This can be an extremely positive parenting style, as the Helper parent is willing to do whatever it takes to ensure their child gets what they need.

However, this can also be a negative parenting style if the Helper parent takes over too much responsibility for raising their child. They may start micromanaging every aspect of their child's life, resulting in a poor sense of self-worth and low self-esteem.

Relationships

This type of person is all about the romantic

97

relationship. They are looking for someone who can show them love and affection, and they will do everything possible to make their partner happy. The Helper thrives on making other people happy, so if their partner needs help with something or just wants to talk about their day, the Helper will be there for them. Twos are attentive, appreciative, generous, warm, playful, and nurturing at their best in a relationship. Twos make their partners feel special and loved. Twos at their worst are controlling, possessive, needy, and insecure.

What Helpers do in stress

When stressed, the Helper will often take on more tasks or responsibilities. They are the go-to person for advice and assistance, which can be helpful when they need to vent or process something emotionally. However, if this behavior becomes a habit, it could lead to burnout and resentment from others who feel the Helper's generosity is taken advantage of.

What Helpers do in peace

When Helpers are at peace, it's time to help others. They can help others by being a good listener, a shoulder to cry on, and being there when others need them.

Type Three: The Achiever

Traits

Ambitious and focused on results, Achievers encourage others to be the best they can be. They might have problems being too focused on appearances or adjusting who they are, depending on who is around at the time. At their best, they are competent, enthusiastic, and accomplished. They want to be accepted, valued, successful, and respected for their work. They strive to be celebrated for their achievements, and they want to celebrate others as well. It's important to them to be the best at what they do and to be accepted for who they are.

Achievers push themselves and others to improve and are willing to do whatever it takes to succeed. They have a strong sense of right and wrong and feel very strongly about their morals. They believe in being loyal and honest and expect that same loyalty and honesty from others.

Beliefs

Type Threes want to be celebrated for their

100

achievements. They tend to put aside emotions because emotions can get in the way of what they want to accomplish. They tend to overwork and become at risk for burnout.

Strengths

Achievers are the embodiment of excellence. They deliver superb accomplishments in all aspects, and their impressive style is backed up by substantial achievement. They have a keen eye for detail and are aware of their strengths and weaknesses, allowing them to maximize their performance. They like to have a plan before starting work on something new. They also like when things are organized at work, and there is a clear hierarchy of authority.

Weaknesses

Achievers are addicted to the limelight and will stop at nothing to bolster their self-image. Cut off from their true feelings; they cling to the external trappings of success. They can become ruthless with anyone threatening their position, resorting to underhand methods to discredit them. The Achiever personality type can become frustrated if the rules keep changing or if there is a lack of structure in the workplace.

Desires

Type Threes have a fundamental desire to feel valuable and worthwhile. They tend to be very ambitious and always look for ways to reach the next level at work. They can be very competitive, but they also want to ensure their fair approach. This type is a doer. They love to get things done, and they are always busy. They are not afraid of hard work and don't mind getting their hands dirty. They may be impulsive, but they're also highly ambitious.

Fears

Achievers tend to see themselves as the leader of whatever project they undertake. They have a natural drive toward accomplishment and success and always have high expectations for themselves and those around them. They fear being worthless or undervalued.

Work and Career

Achievers are hardworking, goal-oriented, organized,

and decisive. They are passionate about their work. They love to achieve their goals and enjoy being recognized for their efforts. These people are also very good at working in groups because they know how to motivate others and encourage them to action. They are frequently in management or leadership positions in business, law, banking, the computer field, and politics.

Leadership Style

Achievers often take on leadership positions within organizations because of their strong work ethic and ability to motivate others through example. They're also very social—they love being around people and can be quite charming when they want to be. Achievers can be excellent managers because they are good at delegating work, organizing projects, and motivating others to get tasks done.

Parenting Style

The Achiever is a parent who's all about setting goals, achieving them, and then setting some more. These parents are great at ensuring their kids are doing well in school, but they can sometimes be too overbearing.

103

They can also be perfectionists and have high expectations for everyone around them.

Relationships

Achievers tend to be very dependable in their relationships with others. This can lead to positive romantic relationships and friendships. Achievers at their best in a relationship value and accept their partners. They are playful, giving, responsible, and well regarded by others in the community. At their worst, they are preoccupied with work and projects. They are self-absorbed, defensive, impatient, dishonest, and controlling.

What Achievers Do when feeling stress

The Achiever is the type of person who thrives on competition and challenge. They can handle pressure, but they need to be able to see the end goal to feel motivated.

When faced with stress, the Achiever tends to focus on the task at hand and tries to get it over with as quickly as possible. They may also work harder than usual to prove something to themselves or others.

What Achievers do when in Peace

When the Achiever is feeling happy, they will be doing something productive. They are always looking for ways to improve their lives, and they will use this happiness to ensure they continuously improve themselves as much as possible. They will seek new goals and challenges to conquer because they have an insatiable desire to grow and improve themselves.

Type Four: The Individualist

Traits

Creative and focused on aesthetics, Individualists tend to encourage authenticity and self-expression, both physically and emotionally. They might have problems comparing themselves to others, extreme sensitivity to criticism, and might be seen as self-absorbed. At their best, they are empathetic, caring, and highly intuitive to others' feelings. They want to make a significant impact and to have a unique identity that allows them to truly feel like themselves. They fear being seen as defective, like something is wrong with them, or having no identity. They strive to always see the beauty in everything and only to have deep and meaningful connections with others. It's important to them to truly be seen, heard, and understood. Individualists are motivated by the need to experience their feelings and be understood, search for the meaning of life, and avoid being ordinary.

Beliefs

Fours are highly sensitive to their own emotions, able to introspect deeply and express these feelings in

106

original ways. Fours take their identity from their sense of being true to themselves and following their own path in life. They constantly look for deep connections and meaningful experiences. They often compare what they have (or don't have) to others.

Individualists tend to be introverts who need lots of alone time to recharge their energy levels. They enjoy spending time with others when they can connect on a deep level—otherwise, they'd rather spend time alone than with persons that don't make them feel valued or heard.

Strengths

Individualists are described as creative and artistic and can often see things in a unique way that allows them to be very successful at whatever they do. They can also be highly intuitive to others' feelings. They can inspire others with their originality. Instead of being attached to their feelings, they enjoy expressing them and touching others' hearts.

Weaknesses

Individualists are often very sensitive people who have

107

difficulty not taking things personally—even if someone tries to be kind. Because Individualists often feel like an outsider or don't fit in with society at large, they tend to spend a lot of time reading books or watching movies that explore themes related to being different from others or feeling misunderstood by those around them.

They also tend to suffer from high levels of anxiety and depression due to their sensitivity toward other people's needs—which can cause problems if they're not careful. They're also very self-critical and tend to beat themselves up over mistakes or perceived flaws in their character or appearance.

Fears

Individualists tend to be perfectionists who can become easily discouraged when things don't go according to plan. They often feel like they're not good enough and spend much time worrying about what other people think of them.

Desires

Type Fours' ideal self is often a philanthropic visionary

108

who cares deeply about their family, friends, and the greater good. They want to be known for their humanitarianism and generosity, not just for their material possessions or achievements in life.

The Individualist is not particularly interested in working for others and may have trouble sticking with one company for a long time. They are more interested in pursuing their own goals and may feel most productive when they do so on their own.

Work and Career

Individualists will take a job that doesn't pay well to work with people they love or who share their values. They want to be in an environment where they can feel comfortable being themselves, so it's essential for them to find a career that fits their personality. They enjoy working at jobs where they can make their own decisions, which is why many do well as entrepreneurs or freelancers. Type Fours also enjoy working in creative fields such as art and design, and they tend to be drawn toward jobs that involve helping people in some way (like therapy or social work).

Leadership Style

The Individualist is a natural leader. They are confident, ambitious, and driven. They lead others through inspiration and encouragement. They are good at delegating tasks and empowering others to do their best work. They are also great at inspiring others with their vision of the future. The Individualist is not afraid of making difficult decisions or significant changes in order to see their dream come to life. There isn't much that can stop them when they set their mind on something!

Parenting Style

The Individualist parent has a parenting style focused on the child's needs. The Individualist parent believes that a child should learn from their own mistakes rather than having everything done for them or being told exactly what to do. The Individualist parent is not concerned with how much time they spend with their children but rather what they are doing with that time. They want to ensure their children are provided with opportunities and experiences that will help them become independent thinkers who can navigate life independently.

The Individualist parent does not believe in giving their children too much praise or attention, as this can lead to them having a sense of entitlement or feeling like they are entitled to special treatment. Instead, the Individualist parent focuses on helping their child find their own identity and develop into independent adults who can accomplish things without needing constant support from others.

Relationships

Type Fours are empathetic, supportive, gentle, playful, passionate, and witty at their best in a relationship. They are self-revealing and bond easily. They're often misunderstood and don't always get along with other people. Their pride and unwillingness to compromise can make forming healthy relationships difficult.

Individualists will never be satisfied with a partner who wants to control them or tries to pressure them into doing something they don't want to do. They want a partner who respects their autonomy and encourages them to do whatever makes them happy.

What Individualists do when feeling stress

When stressed, the Individualist will often withdraw from social settings and spend more time alone. Type Fours who experience stress tend to avoid conflict and confrontation and become even more introverted and quiet.

What Individualists do when feeling peace

When feeling happy, the Individualist is likely to be more self-focused and less concerned about others. They may not want to be around others and may even withdraw from some of their social connections. Individualists might feel more aware of themselves, their unique identity, and their appearance when feeling happy. They might spend more time looking in mirrors or trying on different clothes.

Type Five: The Investigator

Traits

Independent and focused on intellect, Investigators tend to learn everything there is to know about a topic. They may spend more time observing life than fully participating in it. At their best, they are dependable, understanding, and objective. They are a great sounding board for others and are genuinely self-sufficient. They want to be knowledgeable and competent. They strive always to understand the world and everyone in it. It's important to them that people respect and honor their boundaries.

The Investigator is the most introverted of all the personality types, and they are also the most likely to be misunderstood by others. They are highly independent and self-sufficient, which makes them great at leading and managing teams. They are not necessarily shy or withdrawn—they just enjoy their own company and need time alone to recharge.

This type spends a lot of time thinking about patterns, connections, and how things relate to one another—

what makes them similar? How do they differ? What can be learned from studying those relationships? They're also interested in how these patterns apply to themselves and their lives; they want to learn more about themselves to become better people.

Beliefs

Type Fives love learning new things about science and technology but also enjoy learning about history, art, and other subjects that help them understand their place in the universe. The key to working well with an Investigator is to give them space when needed and ensure they know that you value their unique perspective.

Investigators enjoy new experiences and exploring unfamiliar territory. They love puzzles, riddles, and mysteries—they may even be obsessed with solving them! Investigators tend to be logical thinkers who enjoy examining facts and data from different angles to reach an accurate conclusion.

Strengths

Investigators are gifted with focused concentration

and deep thought, analyzing a problem, topic, or situation and reaching reasoned conclusions. They are reflective thinkers who like to explore their surroundings. They seek knowledge and information about the world around them and enjoy learning new things. They tend to be very intelligent, curious people who always try to improve themselves and their surroundings. Investigators can also be very creative, as they have a rich inner world that they draw from when solving problems or coming up with new ideas.

Weaknesses

Investigators can be quite reserved when sharing their feelings with others, preferring to internalize their emotions and keep them private. Problems arise when thinking becomes a substitute for action and when they get so used to 'living in their heads' that they lose touch with their own feelings and become insensitive to others. They also might have problems with being seen as arrogant, withdrawn, or stingy with their time and resources.

Fears

Type Fives fear being incapable of doing something

and having their energy depleted. They also fear being helpless, useless, incompetent, or overwhelmed.

Desires

People with this personality type tend to be very independent individuals who want to make changes in society. They thrive on being able to help others by giving them access to more information or by improving their education system so they can learn more effectively.

These people are the ultimate seekers of knowledge. They're constantly searching for deeper meaning and greater understanding, whether it's about themselves or what's going on in the world. These people continuously ask questions and seek answers to satisfy their thirst for understanding.

Work and Career

The Investigator is a true entrepreneur and loves to tinker with new ideas and concepts. They're constantly searching for ways to improve their lives and the lives of others. They are on a constant quest for knowledge, which can lead to some pretty intriguing discoveries!

The Investigator is often drawn to careers that give them the freedom to explore and create—but they aren't afraid of hard work either. They enjoy challenges, even if those challenges require lots of research, practice, and patience before they achieve their goal. They usually like to work alone, are independent thinkers, and often in scientific, technical, or other intellectually demanding fields.

Leadership style

Investigators are natural leaders, but they're not the kind of people who will just take control and make decisions on their own. They prefer to take in information from all angles, then decide what's best. They're good at taking charge when needed, and they know how to be a good listener when needed. Their natural curiosity makes them excellent problem-solvers, perfecting them for leadership positions in business or organized sports teams.

The Investigator is an analytical and focused leader who likes to take their time. They are generally quite good at delegating and planning but sometimes feel overwhelmed by their team's demands. They need to remember that it's okay to let others make mistakes and that they don't have to be involved in every little detail.

Parenting Style

The Investigator is an introvert, and their approach to parenting is likely to be very different from the other parenting styles. They will be concerned with keeping their child safe, but they will also want to understand how that child's personality fits into the world around them. The investigator believes in letting children develop independently while being there as a support system when needed.

Relationships

Investigators are quite curious and concerned with the details of their relationships. They like to know everything about their partner, their past and present. Their curiosity can sometimes be intrusive, but it is usually motivated by a desire to understand their partner better. They tend to be very loyal and devoted partners.

Type Fives' investigative nature means they'll always

have new things to learn about their partners, which keeps things fresh and exciting. They are also very loyal, which makes them an ideal partner.

What Investigators do when feeling stressed

When stressed, Investigators tend to get stuck in their heads. They'll obsess over problem-solving, which can be helpful when it comes time to move forward with a plan of action but can also be a bit exhausting. Suppose an Investigator feels overwhelmed by their stressors. In that case, they might need to take a break from thinking about themselves to recharge and prepare for another problem-solving round.

When Investigators feel overwhelmed, they often ask themselves these questions: What is the problem? What do I know about this problem? Who else could help me with this situation?

What Investigators do when in Peace

When feeling happy, the Investigator often does a quick mental review of what has been going well for them lately. They may also take note of any small things that have gone wrong and try to resolve them quickly. The Investigator will also take this time to think about future plans and goals so that they can start working toward them immediately after the feeling passes.

Type Six: The Loyalist

Traits

Community-oriented and focused on stability, Loyalists tend to always be prepared and think things through. They might have problems with worst-case scenario thinking, anxiety, or pessimism. They are courageous and responsible at their best and have a strong sense of humor. They want support, guidance, and security from the people and environment around them. They typically fear being left alone without help, guidance, or protection. They strive to always plan for what could happen and be prepared for whatever comes their way. It's important to them to have a commitment from others.

Those with Six personality types are known for their loyalty, compassion, and generosity. They are always ready to help others and give of themselves. They would rather suffer than see other people suffer. People with type Six personalities are often calm and collected but can also be sensitive and emotional. They are typically excellent listeners who can put others at ease because of their kindness.

121

Beliefs

Type Sixes tend to be very aware of the needs of others and often do whatever they can to ensure those needs are met. They will go out of their way to help someone in need and often feel guilty if they don't do anything.

Strengths

Loyalists are often responsible for taking care of others in their lives—whether it's their family members or someone at work who needs support during difficult times. The Loyalist is often seen as a pillar of strength because they have such an ability to empathize with others. They can keep a clear head even when alert for danger and see potential threats in perspective, responding appropriately. They are happy to work tirelessly in the background without needing special recognition.

Weaknesses

Loyalists are suspicious and volatile, quick to accuse, and slow to trust or forgive. Their alertness spills over into paranoia. This personality type is also susceptible to criticism and often takes things too personally.

Loyalists have a strong desire to be loved and accepted by others, but this can lead them into unhealthy relationships with people who take advantage of their kindness or generosity. They often think about what could go wrong and plan accordingly.

Fears

Loyalists are committed to their beliefs and values and can get very defensive when they feel those beliefs are threatened. They may feel that they have been betrayed in some way if someone tries to convince them to change their mind about something. This can sometimes make them appear inflexible or unwilling to compromise.

Desires

Sixes tend to be easy-going and compassionate, and they like to help others. They aim to create a harmonious environment where everyone feels safe and happy. They have a desire to find security and support.

Work and Career

The Loyalist is the type of person who would rather work for an organization than start their own. They are a team player and thrive in environments where they can learn from others and grow their skills. Loyalists tend to be more conservative, but they're not rigid— they're focused on being loyal to their company or organization first and foremost.

Leadership style

Loyalists are also known for being great leaders because they can see the big picture while still paying attention to details. When it comes to leading, they're very good at communicating with people at all levels of an organization without making anyone feel inferior.

The Loyalist's leadership style is straightforward and honest—they tell people what they need to hear, even if it's difficult. They ensure everyone understands their roles in the project or organization to succeed at their jobs and feel good about what they're doing daily.

Parenting Style

The Loyalist parent is the type of parent who wants their children to know that they will always be there for them, no matter what. They are willing to do whatever it takes to ensure their children are happy and safe and put their needs aside to ensure that happens. The Loyalist parent is usually very close with their children and often relies on them for advice or help with difficult decisions. The Loyalists will go out of their way to make sure their child feels supported by them, even if it means putting themselves in harm's way or giving up something important.

Relationships

In relationships with others, the Loyalist tends to be very patient and understanding of others' needs and wants. They also are people who like giving back as much as they get from others—whether through volunteering at charitable organizations or helping out friends when they're having trouble at work or school.

Loyalists at their best in a relationship are warm, playful, open, loyal, supportive, honest, fair, and reliable. They are suspicious, controlling, inflexible, and sarcastic at their worst. They either withdraw or put on a tough act when threatened.

What Loyalists do when feeling stressed

People with type Six personalities are known for being loyal and devoted to others and highly cautious and skeptical. When stressed, they may turn inward, withdraw from the world, or take on more responsibilities at work or home. They want to ensure that everything is perfect in their lives to feel safe and secure.

What Loyalists do when in Peace

When feeling happy, a type Six will take a moment to reflect on their life and feel grateful for all the good things in it. They will look at the people in their lives who have positively impacted them and be thankful for those relationships.

Type Seven: Enthusiast

Traits

The Enthusiast is a natural-born leader. They are charismatic, energetic, and inspiring. They love to be the center of attention and can often be found organizing events or activities for their friends and family. They are driven, competitive, and extremely ambitious. They can be both charming and charmingly irreverent. They have a strong sense of humor and love to tell jokes; they're also very good at making people laugh. Sevens often have a wide circle of friends, many of whom are quite different from each other.

Beliefs

Enthusiasts often see the world through rose-colored glasses. People come to them to be cheered up or to help them look on the bright side. They cannot sit still because they always want to move on to the next thing. They might also be enthusiasts of specific causes, like saving animals or helping people in need. One thing that really makes them happy is being able to help someone else out by donating time or money. They're also very energetic and active, so it's no surprise

127

they're big fans of sports and exercise! If they could do anything right now, it would probably involve getting outside or finding some way to get moving around.

Strengths

The Enthusiast is an excellent communicator who thrives on social interaction. They are also incredibly loyal to their loved ones, standing by them through thick and thin, even if it means being dragged into a situation they disagree with. The power of positive thinking and the ability to see interesting ideas and positive possibilities anywhere.

Weaknesses

Type Sevens love having people around them, especially those they like. Still, they may have difficulty expressing their feelings when they feel rejected by others or left out of the conversation.

Fears

Enthusiasts fear being controlled by others, which motivates them to stand up for themselves and speak their minds. They don't like being told what to do; they

128

want everyone to leave them alone so they can do what they want.

Desires

Type Sevens are enthusiastic and energetic. They have a strong desire to make the world a better place, and they don't let anything get in the way of their pursuit of that goal. They can be accommodating but also be bossy and "know-it-all-ish".

Work and Career

Type Sevens are the type of people who love to work. They're passionate about their careers and will do whatever it takes to get ahead. They'll push themselves and those around them to achieve success. They have high expectations for themselves and their coworkers, and they're quick to point out flaws in the system or where someone has slipped up. They thrive on competition and always look for ways to improve their performance or that of others. They may not always be as vocal about their opinions as some other types, but they are still committed to being recognized as valuable employees by their employers.

Leadership style

Enthusiasts will often find themselves in leadership roles because of their ability to draw others in with their charisma and infectiously positive attitude. However, they can sometimes struggle to balance their responsibilities as a leader with their need for personal space; if this becomes too much for them, they might start showing signs of passive-aggressive behavior toward other group members.

Parenting Style

The Enthusiast parent is a big believer in focusing on the positive and will always look for ways to make things fun. They want their child to enjoy learning, and they don't like seeing them get upset. Enthusiasts are, as the name suggests, enthusiastic about everything. They live in the moment and love to play, especially with their children. Enthusiasts are often drawn to being a parent because of the opportunity to have fun with another human being. They have an easy time relating to other people, and they can connect with their children in a way that makes them feel safe and secure.

Relationships

Enthusiasts are lighthearted, generous, outgoing, caring, and fun at their best in a relationship. They introduce their friends and loved ones to new activities and adventures. They're usually good at finding humor in situations where other people would just get mad or frustrated. Enthusiasts at their worst are narcissistic, opinionated, defensive, and distracted. They are often hesitant about being tied down to a relationship.

What Enthusiasts do When Feeling Stressed

For a personality type Seven, an Enthusiast, one of the things that they're most likely to feel stressed about is other people's stress. They can't stand seeing those around them upset or struggling and are always looking for ways to help. But here's the thing—in many cases, others' problems are outside of their control. And that can be incredibly frustrating.

What Enthusiasts do When in Peace

When type Sevens are happy, they want to share that joy with everyone around them. They're excited about life and want to spread their enthusiasm for it wherever they go. When they feel like this, they need to take advantage of the fact that so many people will appreciate their enthusiasm and want to be around them. So they should go out and meet new people, go to a party, or join a club or group that interests them.

Type Eight: The Challenger

Traits

Decisive and focused on protecting themselves and others, Challengers tend to stand up for others and cheer on the underdog. They might have problems with being quick to anger, aggressive, and intimidating. At their best, they are influential, decisive, and passionate. They are also very honest, even when the truth hurts. They want to be able to control their situation and environment and determine the next steps by themselves. It's important to them to fight against injustices and to protect the vulnerable.

Beliefs

People with this personality type are known for their courage, determination, and fearlessness. They are driven to protect others and ensure they're safe. They love to be challenged and thrive in situations where they can be relied on. They can quickly make decisions without much thought. They feel comfortable debating and dealing with conflict. They wish other people could stand up for themselves as they do.

Strengths

Type Eights see themselves as leaders and pillars of strength, with a duty to guide and protect weaker individuals. Because of their confidence in themselves and their judgment, they have no hesitation in placing themselves 'in the firing line' for the good of the group. They possess a powerful presence full of physical vigor and are not afraid to take the lead and act decisively.

Weaknesses

Type Eights have a strong sense of right and wrong, which can sometimes make them judgmental. They also tend to be focused on getting the job done and can become aggressive if they feel they're being blocked from achieving their goals. They also don't like being stuck in a rut and want to push themselves and grow constantly.

Fears

Challengers fear being seen as weak or being controlled or harmed by others. They strive to avoid vulnerability because that can be perceived as weakness. They can become intoxicated with power and more concerned with fighting off contenders than serving the group.

Desires

Type Eights strongly desire to improve themselves and the world around them. They tend to be competitive and driven by their need for achievement. Challengers are often good at managing crises and can easily handle complex tasks. They don't need a lot of guidance or direction to get things done, but they need someone to trust them with important decisions.

Work and Career

The Challenger is the person who is always ready to take on the next challenge. This type of person thrives on competition and loves to win. They are not afraid to fail as long as they learn from their mistakes. They are willing to go the extra mile for their job and do whatever it takes to get it done. When working with this type of person, you can expect them to be highly motivated and driven individuals who will always put 110% effort into everything they do.

Leadership Style

The Challenger is a natural-born leader. They are confident, charismatic, and driven—and they know it. They are not afraid to take risks or push boundaries and love the thrill of being in charge. Of course, this doesn't mean that Challengers don't make mistakes. They do! But they're also incredibly resilient and can bounce back from their mistakes more quickly than other types of people might be able to.

Challengers tend to be very goal-oriented in work and play—they have an insatiable drive for achievement that makes them the best leaders out there.

Parenting Style

The Challenger is a parent who believes their child should be able to stand on their own two feet. They have high expectations for their child and don't believe in coddling or protecting them from the realities of life. They are more likely to be the one who tells their child they're grounded or the one who calls them out when they've done something wrong.

Relationships

Type Eights are known for their ability to get things done, but they also make great companions. They're loyal and protective of their loved ones and enjoy being part of a group or community. Type Eights are also known for having an intense sense of humor, which can help keep the peace in any relationship. At their worst, they can be demanding, arrogant, combative, possessive, uncompromising, and quick to find fault.

What Challengers do when feeling stressed

When type Eights are stressed, it's essential for them to remember that the only thing they have control over is their own self. If a Challenger is feeling overwhelmed, they should take a moment to breathe and try to remember their default state of mind.

What Challengers do when in peace

If type Eight is happy, they want to share this joy with everyone around them. But sometimes, they need to sit with their emotions and enjoy them for a little while before sharing them with others.

137

Type Nine: The Peacemaker

Traits

Patient and focused on making sure everyone else is okay, Peacemakers tend to go with the flow and offer nonjudgmental perspectives. They might have problems with decision-making, not speaking up when they have a thought or opinion, or becoming passive-aggressive. At their best, they are kind, generous, and open with their feelings. They want to maintain their inner peace and stability. They strive to see all sides of a situation and to be open and accepting of everyone. It's important for them to take the time to relax and focus on cultivating important relationships.

Beliefs

Type Nines enjoy being around other people and dislike conflict. They are very diplomatic and try to see the good in everyone. They can be quite generous but also have trouble saying no when people ask for favors or advice. They are very loyal, especially when their friends or family members need help with something important to them.

Strengths

The strength of type Nine is their ability to see both sides of an issue or problem. This allows them to find common ground between two opposing viewpoints or parties. They are excellent mediators because they can see both sides clearly without prejudice.

Weaknesses

They don't like confrontation, and instead of confronting someone directly about something that bothers them, they will go out of their way to avoid the situation instead (not always an easy task). They also have a difficult time asking for help when they need it (which is often). Because of their ability to blend with a group, they sometimes seem to merge into the background and do not always receive due credit. Problems arise when their habitual focus on the group leads them to neglect their own needs and to hesitate when decisive action is called for.

Fears

Peacemakers fear conflict more than anything. This is because people with a type Nine personality are afraid of losing or being abandoned by those close to them. This means they fail to speak up or take action when it is called for, and as a result, problems fester, and critical issues are neglected.

Desires

Peacemakers have a fundamental desire for inner stability, "peace of mind." Their passion for peace is strong enough to motivate them toward success in all aspects of their lives.

Work and Career

Type Nines are natural diplomats and peacemakers keen on getting people to work together. They tend to be very patient, fair, and easygoing. They're unlikely to make waves or rock the boat. They're also unlikely to be in a position of power because they don't want to upset anyone or make decisions that will negatively impact others. Instead, they'd rather help everyone come together as a team and reach an agreement that everyone is comfortable with.

Leadership Style

Peacemakers can see all sides of an argument or situation, so it's no surprise that many Type Nines become leaders in their field. They have great vision, empathy, and compassion—qualities that make them excellent leaders.

Parenting Style

Type Nines are not likely to be controlling parents. They are more likely to have a laid-back approach to parenting—they believe in letting their children figure things out themselves, but they'll be around if needed for advice or guidance.

Relationships

The relationship between a Nine and their partner is marked by peace, harmony, and almost childlike trust. This is because the Nine has a deep-seated belief that the world is inherently good and that people are inherently good—and they want to help ensure it stays that way.

They're likely to support their partner's goals and

dreams as long as those goals aren't too big for them to handle. If a partner is too ambitious or trying to take on too much, the Nine will try to get them to see reason or calm down.

Nines at their best in a relationship are kind, gentle, reassuring, supportive, loyal, and nonjudgmental. At their worst, they are stubborn, passive-aggressive, unassertive, overly accommodating, and defensive.

What Peacemakers do when feeling stress

A Peacemaker is most likely to feel stressed if they feel like their life is out of control. They hate feeling like things are messy and want to keep everything neat and organized.

No matter what kind of stress you're feeling, if you're a type Nine, here's how to deal with it:

- Take a step back and look at your situation from a distance. Ask yourself if there's anything you can do about it right now. If not, just wait until something needs to be done and then go back to it.

- Go for a walk or run to clear your head and get some exercise in. It will help increase blood flow and release endorphins—the chemical in your brain that makes us feel good!

What Peacemakers do when in peace

Type Nines are Peacemakers. They love feeling connected to other people and helping them find their inner peace. They love being able to make others happy by helping them solve problems and heal their relationships.

When a Type Nine is happy, the best thing they can do is share that happiness with others. They'll reach out to their friends, family members, or coworkers and ask what they can do for them. They'll offer advice and support when needed—and if someone needs help making a decision or solving a problem, they'll be there with open arms!

CHAPTER 4: THE HEAD, THE HEART, AND THE BODY.

The Enneagram is a system of personality types developed in the early 20th century by the Greek mystic George Gurdjieff and his student, Oscar Ichazo. The Enneagram has been described as a "universal law of spiritual being" or "a map of the soul."

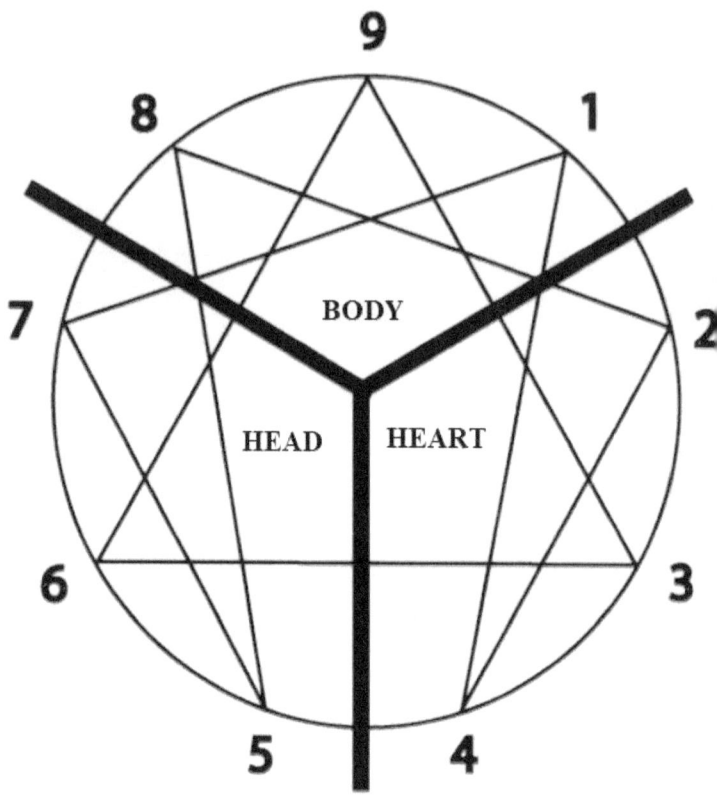

The 3 Centers (Triads)

The wisdom tradition behind the Enneagram holds that humans are "three-brained beings"— we function through three different "centers of intelligence" - emotional, mental, and physical. Each center has its unique way of processing information and making

146

decisions, which forms our personality type.

The three centers of intelligence correspond to three different aspects of our personalities:

- The first center is our body center, which allows us to take action, get into motion, experience our physical sensations, and exert control of our environment. It guides when to take action and when not to take action. It helps us to experience life around us and get things done kinesthetically.
- The second center is our heart center, which allows us to experience our feelings, connect with others emotionally, and be sensitive to their emotional reactions. It helps us relate to other people and form and maintain relationships in our lives.
- The third center is our head center, which allows us to gather and analyze information, brainstorm new ways of doing things, and make plans for the future. It helps us experience and express our thoughts and beliefs and perform

other cognitive tasks like visualization and imagination.

As human beings, we process things through all three of these, but the center in which your Enneagram number lands shows you which way of processing you naturally lean on the most.

The three centers of intelligence are an essential foundation to the Enneagram. These centers provide a range of information that helps us understand our own type's gifts and challenges and why other types see the world so differently. They also provide a way to create greater balance within yourself as part of your everyday growth practice.

Body Center - What do I need to do?

Enneagram Types: Eight, Nine, and One

The Body or Instinctive center is home to enneagram types 8, 9, and 1. While these numbers seem different, they share the same gut instincts. These types tend to be impacted primarily by their deep instincts and

148

innate anger. They each have a desire for independence and control over their own environment.

Types in the Body center can be strong, stable, grounded, and connected with life when healthy. These types' strength lies in their intuitive intelligence - their ability to tune into their 'gut feeling' about people and situations, commit to action, and see it through with grit and determination. The common emotion for the Body center is anger.

They become overly focused on their physical sensations as a way to react and respond to the world. They use their body as a way to control their immediate environment and to help them achieve whatever their primary goal is. And because they are focused on taking direct action.

All Body center types focus on being practical, quickly seeking out the one right way to do things and get them done. People in this center tend to put their practical wants and needs in the background. They struggle with control issues more than the other six Enneagram types. They want to affect the world, but not be affected by it. While all three share this same struggle, they each do something different to solve their need for control.

For Body types, once they are in motion, they can find it very hard to stop—especially if that action has become automatic or programmed. Body types find it easier to take action now and analyze later (if at all). And they find it challenging to slow down and get into their feelings.

Head Center - What do I think?

<u>Enneagram Types: Five, Six, and Seven</u>

The Head center types relate to reality through logical and analytical reasoning. Their strength lies in their mental intelligence - their ability to think clearly, penetrate deeply into a subject or create new action options. They each are likely to be fearful or insecure, particularly in less healthy times, and may feel like their mind is overactive and noisy. Head types can be wise, creative, and thoughtful at their best. However, their fear can wreak havoc if they don't learn to process

150

and address it healthily. The common emotion of the head center is fear.

They spend a lot more time thinking than other types. They are constantly scanning the room for possible issues and creating different scenarios for how they could respond.

People in this center tend to focus on safety and security. They struggle with finding a sense of inner guidance and support. They are always seeking to find safety and security, which they lack internally more than the other six numbers.

Head types struggle to take action on their ideas and can procrastinate for hours, days, or months on something they want. They also find it hard to access their heart and connect with their feelings as well as the feelings of others.

The Heart – What do I feel?

Enneagram Types: Two, Three, and Four

The heart is the symbol of love and compassion.

Enneagram types of this center's strength lie in their emotional intelligence - their ability to relate to others and their own emotions. They all want to feel affirmed and appreciated by other people, whether they are aware of it or not. When they're healthy, heart types can be caring, authentic, and connected with others. However, they may express shame negatively when they don't take the time to work through it properly. The common emotion in the heart center is shame.

The heart is the energy center of your body. It represents your emotions, where you feel love, joy, happiness, and all those other positive feelings that make life worth living. But it also houses negative emotions like anger, jealousy, and sadness.

People in this center try to gain approval from others. They struggle with the lack of a sense of their own identity more than other numbers. They are always looking to shed their false self and discover who they really are. While all three share this same struggle, they each do something different to solve their search for identity.

Heart types can find it challenging to sense their own body or to disconnect from their feelings and analyze a situation from different angles.

Which Center Do You Belong?

We developed a preference for one of these centers through our inborn type and childhood development. And the more we used that one center of intelligence, the more we started to believe that it was the only appropriate way to navigate the world.

Jim Gum, founder of Story Enneagram, offers a great illustration of how to decide which center you are in. He shows a video of him that went viral a few years ago, where he is crawling to the edge of a cliff, too scared to look over. Rather than lending a supporting hand, his wife Lee filmed his attempt to reach the edge. He noticed people reacting to this scenario in three different ways, which revealed how the three different centers respond to things differently:

- **Body Center:** People had a visceral reaction. Their stomach dropped, and they felt the fear of being so close to a cliff edge just by watching the video.

- **Heart Center:** People loved the relationship they saw between his wife filming and him crawling. They pointed out the banter and how wonderful they were as a couple. Their hearts were stirred by what they saw.

- **Head Center:** People thought that it made total sense that he was so afraid. Falling off of a cliff that high would kill him. They thought about the danger of the situation.

Do you see how each center reacts to the same scenario in a different way? This illustrates how each center processes things differently. Identifying how you respond to something, whether from your body, heart, or head, can help you narrow down which center your Enneagram number lies in.

A Short Message from the Author

Hi, are you enjoying the book thus far? I'd love to hear your thoughts! Many readers do not know how hard reviews are to come by, and how much they help an author.

I would be incredibly thankful if you could take just 60 seconds to write a brief review, even if it's just a few sentences!

Thank you for taking the time to share your thoughts!

CHAPTER 5: DETERMINING YOUR TYPE

"The Enneagram number you find is not for the sake of mere self-categorization, it is for the enlightenment of the person, by helping them to recognize their own addictive pattern of seeing and thinking." – Richard Rohr

Enneagram teachers typically recommend two ways of working on yourself with the Enneagram. The first is simply to observe your type - read the descriptions and notice when you are compelled to act according to type. For example - if you are Type Two, notice when you feel compelled to help someone; if you are Type Seven, notice when you get bored and feel the need to lighten the mood; if you are Type Five, notice when you feel the need to withdraw from the group and gather your thoughts.

Getting into the habit of 'just observing' yourself is a great way to learn about yourself, even if the observations can sometimes make you uncomfortable. It is a humbling experience to realize how much of our thoughts, feelings, and behavior are conditioned by our type. This can also help us develop compassion for others when we notice that they are also trapped by their type.

Another great way to determine your Enneagram type is through a test or assessment. It's sometimes much harder to be objective about ourselves when we're just sitting around thinking about it. Taking a test or assessment will allow you to explore your personality in a safe space where you can discover new things about yourself.

There are many different tests available online. You

may want to take one of these multiple times to see how your scores change over time.

The Integrative Enneagram Questionnaire (iEQ9)

The Integrative Enneagram Questionnaire (iEQ9) is a tool for helping you explore your Enneagram type. It's an excellent way to better understand yourself and your personality and how that compares to other people in your life. The iEQ9 has 175 questions and is incredibly thorough—it can take anywhere from 15 to 45 minutes to complete.

This is the most comprehensive questionnaire of its kind. The iEQ9 provides much more information than other questionnaires and measures all nine Enneagram types and your shadow side.

The iEQ9 is also much more accurate than other questionnaires because it includes the highest quality items from several well-known questionnaires, including the original MBTI (Myers Briggs Type Indicator), Portrait of Temperament (POT), Socionics

Intertype Relations Questionnaire, and many others. These items have been rigorously tested for reliability and validity using statistical procedures that are standard in psychology today.

The iEQ9 was created by Dr. David Daniels, a highly regarded expert on the Enneagram and its applications in organizational development. It's the only survey of its kind that's been developed by a Ph.D. in any field of psychology—and his work has been featured in the New York Times and other major publications.

It's also a great way to discover how you relate to other people—whether it's your partner or someone else in your life with whom you've been struggling to get along. And it can be used as a tool for self-discovery and growth.

Riso-Hudson Enneagram Type Indicator (RHETI)

You can also take the Riso-Hudson Enneagram Type Indicator (RHETI) or the Quick Enneagram Sorting Test (QUEST) to determine your personality type. The

RHETI is a 140-question test developed by Don Riso and Russ Hudson, two of the world's leading experts on the Enneagram. You can take it through The Enneagram Institute or online at RHETI.com. It takes about 30 minutes to complete.

The QUEST

The QUEST is a free online test developed by Phil Goldberg, another expert on the Enneagram. You can take it at QuestEnneagramTest.com. It takes about five minutes to complete.

Whether you use the Riso-Hudson Enneagram Type Indicator (RHETI) through The Enneagram Institute or the Quick Enneagram Sorting Test (QUEST), there are many reasons to take the test. Here are just a few:

1. Learn more about yourself.

2. Get a sense of how your personality type affects how you interact with others.

3. Understand why some situations make you feel uneasy or uncomfortable, and more easily navigate

161

them in the future.

How to confirm and verify your Personality type

To confirm your personality type, you'll need to take the Enneagram test. This personality assessment will help you understand how you relate to others and how to understand yourself better.

Once you've taken the test, you'll receive an email with your results. If you're unsure if it's accurate, re-read the nine enneagram types in Chapter 3 again for more information on each type and descriptions of their traits.

Confirming and verifying your personality type is the first step in learning more about yourself. This process is the foundation of Enneagram and helps you understand how to use the Enneagram system to improve yourself, your relationships, and your life.

There are two steps to confirming and verifying your personality type:

1) Take one or both of the following quizzes (or find an online version of them) to get a general idea of which types of personalities are most dominant for you:

A) The DISC Model Quiz by Dr. David Kiersey (http://www.davidkiersey.com/personality-testing/disc-model/)

B) The Myers-Briggs Type Indicator (MBTI) Quizzes (https://www.16personalities.com/)

2) After taking either quiz, verify your results by checking them against descriptions and traits found in Chapter 3 that seem to fit with what you discovered while taking the quizzes.

What to do when you have discovered your type

Congratulations! You've just discovered your Enneagram type and are on your way to a more fulfilling life.

Enneagram isn't just about what kind of person you are; it's also about how you can improve yourself. The
163

fact that you've taken the time to find out what your type is proves you're committed to self-improvement, and we can't wait to see how far you go!

When you have discovered your type, it is vital to take a moment and reflect on what this means. First, it is essential to remember that you are not your type. You are still you, the same person you were before you discovered your type. You have just learned something new about yourself. Your type is just one part of who you are—it is not all there is to know about yourself. It was only through taking the Enneagram Test that you were able to discover this information about yourself.

It is also crucial for you to realize that no one else can tell what your type is by looking at or talking with you. Your type does not define who you are as a person; rather, it simply describes certain aspects of how your personality functions in relation to others' personalities.

Finally, if someone asks what your type is, it's okay to say, "I don't know." There really isn't any reason why anyone else would need to know your type unless they are interested in learning more about themselves or their relationships with others in general—and even then, there are other ways for them to learn about those things!

So what do you do when you find out your Enneagram type? Here are some tips:

1. **Learn more about it!** Many books, websites, and resources are available online to help explain what your type means and how to work with other types, so everyone involved feels fulfilled by your interactions.
2. **Find someone who shares the same type as you.** You can use sites like Meetup or Facebook groups to find people who share similar traits with you—you'll be amazed at how much easier it is to connect when there are similarities in personality present!
3. **Don't try too hard**—just be yourself! Being honest about who you are and your needs will help everyone around you.
4. **Soak it in.** Take some time to think about what it means to be your type. Are there any

traits that stand out? How do they relate to other parts of your life? What do they say about who you are as a person?

5. **Embrace it!** It's okay if not everything fits perfectly—there's always room for growth. The point is not to get hung up on being perfect; the point is just to get better at understanding yourself so that you can live more authentically and healthily.

6. **Set goals based on this information.** For example, if being a Nine makes sense for me because I'm an introvert who values harmony over conflict, then maybe some of my goals will be to improve my relationships with others by learning to manage conflict well rather than avoid it altogether.

If you're feeling really brave, you might want to show the description of your type to a trusted friend and ask them whether they think it's accurate - pick your friend wisely, and be prepared for a few hard truths!

Using the Enneagram to Work on Yourself and with Others

The Enneagram is a powerful tool for self-understanding, but it also can help us understand others. When you understand people, you can better communicate with them, and you grow as a person when you communicate with them. The key to using the Enneagram for self-improvement is knowing how your type affects you and others around you so that you can work on improving those areas in which you may need help. The same goes for using the Enneagram in working with others—you see their strengths and weaknesses more clearly by understanding your own.

When communicating with other people, it is important to work with their Enneagram type and not against it. The aim is to recognize and respect, even celebrate, the differences between their ways of being, thinking, and feeling and your own. If you can do this, it will not only make them feel valued and understood, it will make the relationship easier, more fulfilling, and more productive for all concerned.

Often we make mistakes because we don't know what's expected of us or why people act as they do. When we understand our type better and recognize it in others, we can learn from them by watching what works best for them.

The Enneagram can help you:

- Understand why you react the way you do in certain situations.
- Understand how your personality affects your relationships with others.
- Improve relationships by working on yourself and better understanding the people around you.

CHAPTER 6: DISCOVERING YOU

You Deserve to Be Known

You are unique and irreplaceable. You deserve to be seen, heard, and understood. You deserve to have your emotions validated and respected. You deserve to be loved for who you are, not for what you do.

We believe that everyone deserves to be known—and we want to help you get there! You need to know yourself. You need to trust your judgment and know you are worthy of being heard. This will help you take control of your life, strengthen your relationships and achieve more at work.

169

But how do you get there? How do you start down the path of being yourself and believing in yourself? It's simple: by taking control of your life.

We believe in empowerment through education, and that learning new things is the best way to improve your life. That's why the Enneagram exists—to help you become aware of your strengths and weaknesses so that you can work on fixing what needs fixing.

When you understand what makes you "you", you can:

Break free from the mundane

When you understand what makes you YOU, you can break free from the mundane and step into a world where anything is possible.

Find your own path

When you understand who you are—what makes you unique—you can find your own path in life. You can create something new and amazing for yourself. You can connect with people who share your interests and values and build daily relationships that improve your life.

The Enneagram is a one-stop shop for all your personal development needs. It'll help you take control of your life (and our team will be there to support you every step of the way). It'll help strengthen your relationships so that even when it feels like everyone else has it together and everyone else seems to be getting where they want to be, at least you know that things are on track with your closest friends and family.

And it'll give you tools for achieving more at work so that even though the workload never seems to get any lighter, at least you have concrete methods for taking on each task effectively and efficiently. This tool doesn't just stop at helping you develop yourself into a well-rounded person—It also offers services that can help make work easier.

So if it feels like life is constantly throwing obstacles in front of you, and there's nothing you can do about it except keep trying harder... let the Enneagram help!

Discover Your Internal GPS

As a human, it's easy to start feeling lost.

We get so caught up in the hustle and bustle of everyday life that we forget what we really want. The Enneagram is here to help you discover your internal GPS and reconnect with what matters most: YOU!

How do you find your internal GPS?

It's easy: You must become more self-aware and trust the Enneagram system and yourself.

The Enneagram is about movement and change, letting go of fixed identity, and opening up to the possibility of transformation. G.I. Gurdjieff, the teacher who first brought knowledge of the Enneagram to the West, taught that we have two natures – 'Personality,' which is essentially illusory, an image of ourselves that we learn from others; and 'Essence,' our true nature. Gurdjieff's system aimed to help people let go of this false self-image so that their true Essence could emerge.

The point of identifying your Enneagram type is not to put you in a box or stick a label on you - but to show you where the type (your self-image) helps you and where it is getting in your way. By deliberately working 'against' your type, you can open up new perspectives and make changes in long-established habits.

So learn to trust yourself first!

We all have an internal GPS that helps us navigate our lives, but sometimes it can go off course. When that happens, it's essential to learn how to read and adjust your internal map so you can stay on the best path for you. Learning about and understanding your strengths and weaknesses will help you remain clear of pitfalls along the way. You'll also be able to take advantage of opportunities that come your way and make sure you're always headed in the right direction.

Transform Your Life

When you're stuck in a rut, it can be hard to imagine a way out. But when you take steps toward improving your mental health, it really can change everything. And the best part is that YOU get to choose how you do it!

Are you ready to live with more empathy and love?

We know how difficult it can be to feel like you're on the right track in life, but we also know that taking control of your mental health is one of the most important things you can do for yourself. You can live with more empathy and love for others, establish a growth path for yourself that allows you to improve each day, and be the best version of yourself in every situation. You can do this by taking small steps every day that will help you achieve your goals, and by surrounding yourself with people who will encourage you on your journey. Transform your life, and you'll transform the world.

You have all the tools within yourself to make this change happen—you just need to believe in yourself enough to start!

What would it be like to live your life with more empathy and love?

We know that this is a question you've been asking

174

yourself and that you're ready to take the next step. But what does it mean to "live with more empathy and love"? How do you even begin to make that happen?

Well, we have good news—there's an easy way. It all starts with establishing a growth path. We'll walk you through everything you need to know about setting up your growth path so you can start living with more empathy and love today!

Discover how to use the Enneagram for personal growth unique to you.

By identifying your type and learning about it, you can better understand yourself and how you operate in the world. This helps you overcome obstacles and get more out of life.

But what does this have to do with personal growth?

Everything! When we learn about ourselves and how we work as a person, we can achieve our goals and improve our lives in ways we never thought possible.

It's not just about knowing what kind of person you are; it's also about understanding how your personality affects how you interact with others, what motivates you, and how you express yourself.

The Enneagram comprises nine personality types, each of which has its strengths and weaknesses. Once you know your type, it will be easier for you to understand how to use those strengths more effectively and manage your weaknesses more effectively.

It can help you discover how to use your natural talents, embrace things about yourself you don't like, and relate better with others.

CONCLUSION

After you have worked through this process, you will undoubtedly see changes in yourself, just as others will. You will likely be more at peace with yourself, more grounded, and more forgiving of yourself and others.

You're not a one-size-fits-all kind of person. And your journey to self-discovery shouldn't be, either. The Enneagram can help you better understand yourself and others. It's been used by millions of people over the past 40 years—from business leaders to therapists and spiritual teachers—to discover their unique gifts, talents, and needs. The Enneagram invites us to look deeply into the mystery of our true identity. It is meant to initiate a process of inquiry that can lead us to a more profound truth about ourselves and our place in the world. If we use the Enneagram simply to arrive at a better self-image, we will stop the process of uncovering (or, actually, recovering) our true nature. While knowing our Enneagram type gives us critical information, that information is merely an embarkation point for a much more extraordinary journey.

Genuine self-knowledge is an invaluable guardian against such self-deception. The Enneagram takes us places (and makes real progress possible) because it starts working from where we actually are. As much as it reveals the heights we are capable of attaining, it also sheds light clearly and nonjudgmentally on the aspects of our lives that are vulnerable and unfree. Work with the Enneagram starts when you identify your type and begin to understand its dominant traits. While we will recognize in ourselves behaviors of all nine types, our most defining characteristics are rooted in one of these types.

Identifying your Enneagram type can be revolutionary. For the first time in our lives, we may see the pattern and overall rationale for the way we have lived and behaved. At a certain point, however, knowing our Enneagram type becomes incorporated into our self-image and may begin to get in the way of our continued growth.

No matter what type you are, you have all nine types in you to some degree. To explore them all and see them all operating in you is to see the full spectrum of human nature. This awareness will give you far more understanding of and compassion for others because you will recognize many aspects of their particular habits and reactions in yourself.

Furthermore, knowing our type or that of someone else can give us many valuable insights. Still, it cannot begin to tell us everything about the person, any more than knowing a person's race or nationality. In itself, type tells us nothing about the person's particular history, intelligence, talent, honesty, integrity, or character. On the other hand, type tells us a great deal about how we view the world, the choices we are likely to make, the values we hold, what motivates us, how we react to people, and how we respond to stress. As we become familiar with the personality patterns revealed by this system, we more easily appreciate perspectives that are different from our own.

The descriptions of the Enneagram types are universal and apply equally to males and females. Males and females will express the same attitudes, traits, and tendencies somewhat differently, but the fundamental characteristics of the type remain the same. None of the Enneagram types is better or worse than any other—all types have unique assets and liabilities, strengths and weaknesses. However, some types can be more valued than others in a given culture or group. As you learn more about all types, you will see that just as each has unique capacities, each has different limitations.

This book aims to stop the automatic reactions of our personality by bringing awareness to it. We awaken only by bringing insight and clarity to the mechanisms of personality. The more we see the mechanical reactions of our personality, the less identified with them we become and the more freedom we have. That is what the Enneagram is all about!

We hope you find what you're looking for and leave feeling refreshed, energized, and ready to start your Enneagram journey!

Thank you for reading!

One more thing

If you enjoyed this book and found it helpful, I'd be very grateful if you'd post a short review on Amazon. Your support does make a difference, and I read all the reviews personally so I can get your feedback and make this book even better. I love hearing from my readers, and I'd really appreciate it if you leave your honest feedback.

Thank you for reading!

BONUS CHAPTER

I would like to share a sneak peek into another one of my books that I think you will enjoy. The book is titled ***"How to Deal with Stress, Depression, and Anxiety: A Vital Guide on How to Deal with Nerves and Coping with Stress, Pain, OCD, and Trauma."***

Are you tired of wasting your time and energy worrying all the time? Do you see the irrationality of constant worrying, but you can't seem to stop doing it? Are you ready to learn how to deal with anxiety and depression without taking drugs?

This book will walk you through precisely why, how, and what you need to do to stop worrying and start living your life.

Nearly 800 million people worldwide experience

mental illness. Some of the most prominent adverse mental conditions include stress, anxiety, and depression. These issues can affect your psychological and physical health, and when you let them go untreated, they can have longstanding effects on your life and relationships. The more you ignore your mental strife, the harder it becomes to be resilient in the face of hardship, and if you let emotions get out of hand, they can lead to increased mental illness.

Though stress is an inseparable part of our lives, we can easily manage it using simple strategies and techniques. All we need is the willingness to learn these techniques and the ability to take action. Effective stress management is critical to your physical, psychological, and emotional health. It's vital to your overall well-being. This book will show you how to start managing your issues and get relief immediately.

How to Deal with Stress, Depression, and

Anxiety provides a complete framework and a well-rounded set of tools to understand the causes of stress, depression, anxiety and how to overcome it.

Enjoy this free chapter!

Virtually all people experience stress, anxiety, or depression at various points in their lives. One 2017 study suggested that about 792 million people worldwide have formal mental health disorders, with depression and anxiety being the most common conditions. Millions, maybe even billions, of additional people experience subclinical conditions and high levels of stress, so the number of people who deal daily with such issues is quite astounding. When you live with any of these conditions, everyday activities become a challenge, and you may resort to self-sabotaging behaviors, or you feel stuck in place.

As these conditions continue, it only makes you feel worse, both mentally and physically. In the United States, it's been reported that stress affects the mental health of 73 percent of the population, leading to worsening conditions like depression and anxiety. While these conditions are all too common, they don't have to be. Living with mental illness or stress can feel impossible, and

186

that's a hard burden to carry, which is why mental distress often leads to further mental and emotional anguish.

The Challenge

With so much external pressure in today's society to be their best selves, millions of people worldwide struggle to maintain their mental health and professional or personal well-being. Many emotionally and physically harmful behaviors—such as overworking and extreme self-sacrifice—are glorified by society. As people are pushed to do their best work and make room for a personal and social life, they can become consumed by anxiety and worries that impede their progress.

The statistics on stress, anxiety, and depression depict a grim picture. As the most prevalent mental health issue in the United States, according to the Anxiety and Depression Association of America, anxiety impacts over 40 million American adults, representing over 18 percent of the population. Globally, nearly 300 million people have anxiety. People who have anxiety tend to have greater stress levels, and 50 percent of those diagnosed with anxiety will also be diagnosed with depression. Depression rates are also startlingly high, with just under seven percent of the population experiencing major depression at any given time and another two percent experiencing persistent depressive disorder, also known as dysthymia or chronic depression.

Even if you don't have a clinically diagnosed issue, such as depression or anxiety, you likely have some degree of stress that makes it harder to function as you'd like to. The Global Organization for Stress says that 75 percent of people are moderately stressed, and nearly all people experience stress at some point in their lives because of a myriad of contributing factors. With so much mental dysfunction, it's no wonder that some people think they'll never get better, but this grim picture doesn't have to be your reality.

While mental health conditions have the power to destroy and debilitate people—paralyzing them and making it hard to have hope for the future—there are proven techniques anyone can use to improve their mental health and allow greater opportunity for personal development. You do not need to let your stress, anxiety, or depression hold you back anymore.

The solution to managing your mental health isn't easy or quick, but it is effective. With effort and careful attention to a multi-faceted plan, you can make dramatic improvements to your damaged mental health and start investing more energy into things that make you the most gratified. There are several steps you must follow for the best results. When you apply these steps, you can have increased mental clarity, emotional freedom, and confidence. Curing your mental health issues will require you to face everything that scares you and to admit uncomfortable truths. Still, you'll be far better off when you seek help than the nearly 25 million Americans who have untreated mental health conditions. You may not need the same level of care as people with more severe conditions, but you do need help because living with any degree of stress, anxiety, or depression is living with more pain than you need to have.

Treating a mental illness can seem intimidating to many people, but there are several effective methods, and there are ways to treat, if not cure, any mental health condition you may have. With so many adults and children not currently being treated for their mental health issues, it's no wonder that mental health statistics remain so prevalent. Still, with increased awareness and the greater availability of mental health resources, the prognosis for those who have mental illness continues to improve. Alongside this, as these issues become more widely acknowledged and discussed, the stigmas attached to them are beginning to dissipate, which removes some of the shame linked to mental illness, which only exacerbates it. Accordingly, by committing bravely to treatment and opening yourself to increased understanding of mental illness, you create resilience against mental illness and become more proactive in the treatment of these debilitating conditions.

For those of you with any of these issues, you cannot delay treatment. Mental dysfunction of any kind makes it harder to feel joy and, in the worst cases, it can deprive you of your ability to function. More than that, your mental health can also impact your physical health. For example, research has shown that stress increases the chance of someone dying from cancer by 32 percent. The Canadian Mental Health Association says that people with poor mental health are more prone to having chronic physical disorders.

A study from Johns Hopkins University found that patients with a family history of heart disease were healthier when they engaged in positive thinking. Among the participants of the study, those who had a positive outlook were 13 percent less likely to experience a cardiac event. Additionally, they found that, generally, people who have better outlooks live longer.

The Solution

Recovery is a process that isn't always linear, but this book will lay out the basic steps to help get you on the right track. The first step in the process is all about education. Before you can do anything else, you must understand the beast you're trying to slaughter and the sword you'll use to slay it. You'll learn how the brain works and how problems with its wiring can lead to mental dysfunction. You'll also learn how you can rewire your cognitive processes to promote increased mental health.

In the second step of the process, you'll continue your educational journey and gain a more in-depth understanding of what anxiety, stress, and depression are and how they impact the way you function. You'll start to understand how to address each of these issues using essential coping tools.

Once you've learned about each condition, you'll be introduced to one of the most powerful psychological tools for improved mental health: Cognitive Behavioral Therapy (CBT). You'll discover what CBT is and how to use it to address your mental ailments.

Once you understand the founding principles of these conditions and the fundamentals of CBT, you'll learn how to manage your circumstances daily by overcoming roadblocks and reviving your sense of self by shifting your perspective as you begin to think in new ways. You'll start to care for both your body and your mind in life-changing ways. All of these steps will lead to mental clarity and mental liberation.

With all this in mind, it's clear that a person's mental health impacts every part of their life, and without addressing your mental dysfunction, you'll never have the peace of mind you crave. Each day you do nothing about your mental health is another day you deprive yourself of health and happiness. Your mental health should be your priority, because you cannot fully function as a member of society if you're prohibited from doing all the things you love the most.

If you feel like you are losing sight of yourself and your desires because of your stress, anxiety, or depression, it's time to make a change. It's okay to be nervous about the adjustments you will need to make to feel healthier, but remember that being uncomfortable and uncertain is vital because they represent change. If you don't change, you'll never feel better than you do now. Maybe you have learned to live with your pain and worry, but it's time to learn to live without those negative coping mechanisms because they stop you from living your life to the fullest.

While the techniques in this book can help you improve your levels of stress, anxiety, and depression, I recommend seeking professional support to help push you towards your goals.

There are tons of books on this subject on the market, so thank you for choosing this one! "How to Deal with Stress, Depression, and Anxiety" will provide a complete framework and a well-rounded set of tools for you to understand the causes of stress, depression, anxiety and how to overcome it. Please enjoy!

How Your Brain Works

Too many people hurt their recovery journey by working against their minds. They think they can force their brains into submission, and when that doesn't work, they feel like failures. When a change you're trying to make doesn't stick, it is usually because it isn't one your brain is used to. As much as you may want that change, your brain will resist it because unfamiliar things feel unsafe to the human brain. The human brain loves patterns, and it uses those patterns to create your internal mental programming and perceptions of reality. When you understand how your brain works, you can use it to your advantage to create new patterns and reframe your mental state.

Your brain is a powerful force, and it can work in remarkable ways. In facing your worries, doubts, and other negative feelings, you need to understand how your brain functions so you can stop fighting your brain and start working with it.

Your Map of Reality

In 1931, scientist and philosopher Alfred Korzybski established an important metaphorical notion with his statement, "The map is not the territory." He believed that individuals don't have absolute knowledge of reality; instead, they have a set of beliefs built up over time that influence how they perceive events and situations. People's beliefs and views (their map) are not reality itself (the territory). In other words, perception is not reality.

Your brain fills gaps in understanding automatically. This means that when you don't know something, you subconsciously make an estimation based on the information you do know. When you experience worry or sadness, this can be caused by a map of reality that reinforces those ideas. That worry or sadness lingers in your mind and can shape future decisions unless you reshape your perception. Your map of reality will always be an interpretation, but it can be an interpretation that helps you rather than hurts you. You can change your map of reality and make it more productive by addressing your thoughts and beliefs and how they impact your behavior.

Thoughts, Core Beliefs, and Behavior

Beliefs are sets of ideas that individuals use to dictate how they'll behave. A belief is something you think is a fact. You feel so strongly about something that you're almost positive it's true, regardless of how well you can prove it. You may have some doubts from time to time, but, overall, you consistently stick to those beliefs. Beliefs are attitudes that you fall back on, because they provide a sense of security, and they make you feel that certain things are constant, which is why something that makes you doubt your beliefs can be so painful. Your beliefs drive your unconscious, habitual behaviors. They become so ingrained in you that they feel natural and inherently true.

When you have trouble managing situations or

coping with feelings, you automatically turn to your beliefs for help without exerting too much brainpower. Your beliefs help you determine morality, and they help you decide whether people or things are bad or good. Your whole perspective uses a compilation of your beliefs to fill in the parts of your reality you can't fully understand.

Beliefs are formed based on past experiences and the stimuli around us. Most people's core beliefs—the most driving beliefs they have—are established when they're young children. As they grow older, children commonly challenge the beliefs they've been taught as they begin to think more critically and independently. Nevertheless, many children reaffirm the beliefs they were taught rather than disproving them. As adults, they can challenge these beliefs and, by managing their beliefs, they can create a healthier view of the world that's a more realistic map of reality.

Beliefs can be incredibly powerful. For example,

imagine parents telling their children that paperclips are dangerous. Telling a child that paperclips are dangerous seems silly. Nevertheless, when those words go unchallenged, the child will internalize the message, and they might try to avoid paperclips, which could impede their ability to do certain tasks. But as they grow older, the child would likely challenge that belief and overcome the fear of paperclips.

Other beliefs may be harder to debunk. For instance, if a mom tells her child that dogs are dangerous, the child may become afraid of dogs. This fear could continue into adulthood, because the child has learned to be terrified of dogs. Even rational arguments that dogs aren't something to be scared of may still make it hard for that child to believe. After all, dogs, unlike paperclips, do have the potential to bark and bite. The child would be so convinced by the belief that it would be hard for them to break from that mindset.

You may have beliefs that stand in your way and feel so foundational to who you are that challenging them makes you uncomfortable. Nevertheless, you need to contemplate your limiting beliefs.

While thoughts and beliefs may seem similar, there are some profound differences between them that you must acknowledge if you want to have a complete understanding of how your thoughts and beliefs can make or break your mental health. Thoughts help to form your beliefs. When you have the same thoughts repeatedly, they become beliefs. You become so used to the thoughts that they become ingrained in your subconscious, and it becomes hard to imagine that those thoughts aren't true. Accordingly, when you think negatively, you tend to have a more pessimistic outlook.

Not all thoughts are beliefs. The thoughts that come and go through your mind without repetition never become beliefs. Beliefs are a product of habitual thinking. This means that while it may be hard to break them, you can break them by overwriting those negative thoughts with positive ones, which is a practice that many therapies and techniques discussed in this book use to reduce stress, anxiety, and depression.

As you've seen with the map of reality, perception shapes our views, and it also shapes the way we think. Your thoughts build your beliefs, and your beliefs, in turn, build your sense of what's real. Some of your beliefs will empower you to seek success and find happiness, while others will make the world seem like a dark and scary place with no hope. Try to identify the parts of your belief system that cause you to have negative responses.

Your thought patterns have tremendous power to change your life. The simple act of interrupting negative thought patterns can help you begin to make changes. These changes don't happen overnight, and deeply entrenched beliefs may even take months or years to debunk completely, but, when you focus on the thought patterns you want to instill, you start to question the "truths" you blindly believed.

There will be some beliefs you'll want to keep, and those are ones you can build upon and use to your advantage throughout this process. There's no need to get rid of any belief that's constructive because such beliefs are the ones that help you grow. However, be honest about the beliefs that are hurting you. Many people try to rationalize certain beliefs that they feel psychologically unready to call into question. Open your mind and contemplate, "Is this belief hurting me in covert and manipulative ways?" If you struggle even to pose that question about a particular belief, that belief may be a harmful one.

The way you think isn't something that's out of

your control. According to the Massachusetts Institute of Technology (MIT), 45 percent of your daily choices are habitual, meaning they're a product of your subconscious thought patterns and beliefs. You choose what stimuli you feed to your subconscious. When worries or hopelessness begin to fill your head, try saying to yourself, "The world is a place full of opportunity and good things." While it won't feel like saying this is doing anything at first, rewriting your internal monologue can be a powerful first step toward growth.

When you understand how thoughts and core beliefs shape your behaviors, it becomes easier to create a path for growth. You learn that you're in charge of your beliefs, and your thoughts can only have as much control over you as you give them. You may feel helpless against your negative thoughts, but learning to overcome these harmful thoughts and release the power they have over you is the only way to become a happier person. The more you try to avoid the things that make you anxious, stressed, or depressed, the more anxious, stressed, and depressed you'll become.

Cognitive Distortions

While your brain does its best to give you helpful information and create an accurate perception of reality, sometimes it gets a little lost trying to translate what it observes into a sensible perception. Your brain loves to make connections, and sometimes, it will make connections that are overly simplified and don't show the nuance in a situation. This is called a cognitive distortion.

Simple speaking, cognitive distortions are falsehoods that your brain persuades you into believing are true. Cognitive distortions can take a variety of forms, but one common example is polarized thinking. When you think in polarities, you see things as wrong or right, good or bad, or win or lose. After you fail at one task, you may start to think, "I'll fail every task because I can't do anything right." This perception isn't an accurate one, but you become convinced it's true because your brain has pinpointed what it thinks is a pattern.

The problem with cognitive distortions is that they're often shrouded in negativity. They make you expect the worse, and they convince you that you cannot do certain things or that other things are unsafe. Cognitive distortions change your perspective, and they can quickly become harmful to your overall well-being. If you believe false messages, it's hard to make peace with your situation or feel secure. When you feel insecure, your mental health declines, and your doubts start to make it harder to function normally. Anxiety may take hold, and you may feel more stressed as you try to complete tasks. The hardship of your situation may then lead to depression.

Cognitive distortions can also cause you to act in ways that worsen your mental state. For example, someone with an eating disorder may tell themselves, "Not eating helps me," when they lose a couple of pounds. They keep going with harmful behaviors because a faulty pattern was established of believing that an action is "good," even though the behavior, for obvious reasons, is the opposite of helpful.

Likewise, someone with anxiety may say, "Avoiding this task will make me feel calmer," when procrastination only heaps on the pressure and stress of the situation. Delaying the task may have given them a sense of relief before, so they keep doing it. It continues to impair them, but cognitive distortion causes them to keep repeating the same harmful behavior. Cognitive distortions fool you into thinking certain actions are good for you or that they aren't as harmful as they are. Someone may engage in risky behavior and think, "This won't hurt me because it didn't harm me before," when that's not accurate information. People often use these distortions to justify harmful, habitual behaviors that give temporary relief to mental distress, but this causes more problems in the long run.

Negative Thoughts

Negative thoughts can play an influential role in how your brain works because your thoughts help create your map of reality and form your cognitive distortions. It's much easier to give in to negative thoughts than positive ones. People often expect the worst because they're afraid that having hope will lead to disappointment. Negative thoughts are also fueled by the internalization of negative comments that others have made about you in the past. For instance, if your mother tells you that you're ugly, you may start to think you're unattractive until it ultimately becomes a core belief.

Research has shown how much healthier and happier people are when they think positively because the brain responds to the input we give it.

So, you can change your outlook by thinking with more positivity. When you think negatively, you're feeding your brain with information it can use against you; therefore, give it information that will help you instead!

The Role of Trauma

Trauma is a significant part of human life, and it can be one of the largest contributors to adverse mental health outcomes, including increased depression, anxiety, and stress. According to the National Council for Behavioral Health, 70 percent of adults in the United States have experienced at least one traumatic event, which means that 223.4 million people in the United States alone have had trauma. Moreover, among people who seek treatment for mental health issues, 90 percent have gone through trauma. Consequently, if you have trauma, it contributes to some of the issues you may be experiencing.

Trauma is the result of events that cause deep

worry or distress. Traumatic experiences are often those that either threaten a person's life or the life or well-being of those they love.

You can have both physical and emotional trauma. Physical trauma can be a response to accidents, injuries, or other physical events. Physical trauma often can trigger emotional trauma, and the scars from emotional trauma often linger longer than those of physical trauma. Trauma can result from physical, verbal, emotional, or sexual abuse, and children who live in violent environments are at an increased risk for trauma. Some people don't realize they have trauma. They might say, "Oh, well, what I went through wasn't that bad compared to other people." However, trauma doesn't mean you were tortured or injured in unthinkable ways. The death of people you love or contracting a serious disease can also cause trauma. Anything can be traumatic if it makes you feel unsafe, so don't downplay those feelings—accept how you feel, even if you don't think it's "that bad."

When you have trauma that you haven't addressed, you're bound to have increased mental challenges. Trauma alone doesn't lead to mental illness, but it's a major contributing factor, and it drives you to rely on unhealthy coping mechanisms that do you more harm than good.

Trauma changes the way you think, which can impact your decision-making processes and your unconscious thoughts. Trauma makes your brain feel unsafe, and when your brain feels unsafe, it focuses on protecting you from future pain, because that pain could threaten your survival. Even in circumstances that don't usually cause anxiety, you may start to feel threatened, even if you can't logically explain why. When you go through trauma, your brain has a stress response, and that stress response reacts to the trauma by changing your future behaviors in an attempt to protect you.

The stress response involves areas of the brain, including the prefrontal cortex, hippocampus, and amygdala. These areas experience lingering changes when they undergo the intense pressure of trauma. As a result, the way your brain processes information shifts when you experience trauma. Your amygdala becomes more active. This part of your brain is responsible for your flight-or-fight reactions and, when it's overactive, it can make you feel as though you're in danger in non-dangerous situations. It stays on guard because it wants to prevent any potential threats from sneaking up on you.

When your amygdala becomes more active, you may be more prone to feeling stressed, and the hippocampus—the part of your brain that handles short-term memories   may become less active. As a result, you may struggle to differentiate between things that happened to you in the past and things that are presently happening.

Finally, the pre-cortex may shrink, and when it does, you have trouble dealing with your emotions and regulating your thoughts. Many of these changes can be found in people who have post-traumatic stress disorder (PTSD), but anyone with trauma can experience them to a lesser degree.

For obvious reasons, trauma makes it hard for you to be mentally healthy, but it also makes it hard for you to be physically healthy. When your physical health declines, this creates additional causes of anxiety, stress, and depression. Thus, not only can your mental health make your physical health worse, but your physical health can make your mental health worse. The Canadian Mental Health Association reports that people with depression are three times as likely to have chronic pain than people without depression. People who have chronic pain are two times as likely to have anxiety or a mood disorder. Mental and physical health are often dependent on one another, which is why the correlations between the two are so important.

According to statistics, you are more likely to experience health issues such as chronic obstructive pulmonary disease (COPD), heart disease, high blood pressure, cancer, and diabetes when you have trauma. These conditions can all reduce your life's quality or longevity, which can then create even more mental unrest. That psychological turbulence can lead to your physical conditions worsening. You can see how these situations can quickly become bleak for those experiencing them. However, by addressing your trauma, you can reduce the potency of some of these issues.

Trauma, unfortunately, is a normal part of life. For many people, it's challenging to manage, but it's nothing to be ashamed of. Using the strategies in this book, you can learn to become conscious of your trauma and take away the power it has to control your life. Simple techniques like listening to music, establishing a healthy diet and exercise routine, practicing meditation, and admitting you have trauma are just some of the most basic techniques you can use to recover.

Recovery from trauma is painful, but it's one of the most important things you can do for your health because working through trauma allows you to heal your brain and teach it new patterns.

Get Professional Help

Before you do anything, you should seek professional help. Seeing a doctor or a mental health professional can help ensure that you have a support system in place to help you improve yourself.

While this book's techniques can help you improve your levels of stress, anxiety, and depression, some people will still need professional support to help push them toward their goals. Additionally, for some people, these issues may be related to their brain chemistry, which may require medication. To have a satisfactory recovery experience, you must take a holistic approach that ensures you achieve long-lasting results and can learn coping skills that will shape the rest of your life.

Get your full copy today! ***"How to Deal with Stress, Depression, and Anxiety: A Vital Guide on How to Deal with Nerves and Coping with Stress, Pain, OCD, and Trauma."***

BOOKS BY RICHARD BANKS

Assertiveness Training: Learn How to Say No
and Stop People-Pleasing by Establishing
Healthy Boundaries

The Keys to Being Brilliantly Confident and More
Assertive: A Vital Guide to Enhancing Your
Communication Skills, Getting Rid of Anxiety,
and Building Assertiveness

The Art of Active Listening: How to Listen
Effectively in 10 Simple Steps to Improve
Relationships and Increase Productivity

How to Deal With Stress, Depression, and
Anxiety: A Vital Guide on How to Deal with
Nerves and Coping with Stress, Pain, OCD and
Trauma

How to Deal with Grief, Loss, and Death: A Survivor's Guide to Coping with Pain and Trauma, and Learning to Live Again

Develop a Positive Mindset and Attract the Life of Your Dreams: Unleash Positive Thinking to Achieve Unbound Happiness, Health, and Success

How to Stop Being Negative, Angry, and Mean: Master Your Mind and Take Control of Your Life

For the Full Book Listing go to https://author.to/RichardBanksBooks